THE MASTER ARCHITECT SERIES REVISITED

Selected and Current Works

Revised and Reprinted 2002

First published in Australia in 1998 by
The Images Publishing Group Pty Ltd
ACN 059 734 431
6 Bastow Place, Mulgrave, Victoria, 3170
Telephone (61 3) 9561 5544 Facsimile (61 3) 9561 4860
Email: books@images.com.au
Website: www.imagespublishinggroup.com

National Library of Australia Cataloguing-in-Publication Data

Hellmuth, Obata & Kassabaum
Hellmuth, Obata + Kassabaum: selected and current works.

Bibliography.
Includes index.
ISBN 1 87690 776 2.

1. Hellmuth, Obata & Kassabaum. 2. Architecture,
American. 3. Architecture, Modern—20th century.
I. Title. (Series: Master architect series revisited).

720.973

Edited by Steve Womersley

Designed by The Graphic Image Studio Pty Ltd,
Mulgrave, Australia

Film by Mission Productions, Hong Kong

Printed by Everbest Printing Co. Ltd. in Hong Kong/China

IMAGES has included on its website a page for special notices in relation to this
and other publications. Please visit: www.imagespublishinggroup.com

Contents

Introduction

Hellmuth, Obata + Kassabaum:
Global Architecture in a World of Change

By Martin Pawley

Here is a vision of the commercial architectural firm of the future. By historic standards it is big, with perhaps 1,000 architects out of a total staff of 3,000. The firm has a presence in some 50 cities around the world, with every office linked via the space–time continuum of electronic communications. Of the firm's architects, perhaps two-thirds are full partners with considerable freedom of action in the service of their clients. They travel extensively, while production staff, housed in computerized facilities, exchange problems and solutions, codes and calculations across time zones via satellite links.

Just as the bare bones of such a firm are recognizable today, so is the nature of its clientele. Corporate- or developer-led, one moment it is expanding, demanding enormous areas of serviced floorspace at short notice; the next it is downsizing according to a preplanned exit strategy that is difficult to reconcile with traditional architectural practice—ancient or modern. This is a difficult, fast moving environment but both architect and clients survive in it because they have learned to live and breathe in an atmosphere of metamorphosis where new buildings are built and old buildings are made over repeatedly, at shorter and shorter intervals. As a result, the firm of the future lives in a world in which terms like old and new, interior and exterior, original function and user function flow into a single concept of perpetual change.

To operate in such a world, the firm of the future has taught itself to mobilize an awesome array of brain power. Overnight it can focus multidisciplinary resources on any one of a wide range of architectural problems, bringing together—virtually or physically—a professional task force ready to undertake the project. To this end, the firm fields not only general-purpose architects but also development strategists, negotiators, planners,

finance people, structural and service engineers, and architects who specialize in areas ranging from health care, residential accommodation, or criminal justice to sports buildings, stadiums and arenas, retail and entertainment environments, corporate and industrial architecture, and so on. Behind this array of talent are further resources based in the firm's offices around the world: there are real estate strategists, product designers, graphic designers, construction administrators, financial feasibility estimators, legal experts, building code analysts, visual communicators, model makers, and many more. This combined task force can undertake anything from predesign programming, through outline and detailed design, costing, code reviews, and construction supervision right up to post-completion surveys. Yet while it is massively expanded in scope from the largest design firms of today, such an organization remains, in essence, architectural because through expertise, experience, organization, and design genius, its contributions to the built environment still constitute an art.

Today, at the end of the 20th century, firms very near to the above description already exist. In 1997, an authoritative survey[1] confirmed the existence worldwide of at least 16 architectural firms billing in excess of US$100 million a year, six of them earning more than 50 percent of their fee income from non-domestic markets. In all but their size, these firms are already configured for global operations.

Although most of them are still tied to their home markets by an umbilical cord of language and tradition, they have long since followed their multinational clients across continental barriers, opening offices in foreign lands wherever demand for their services has justified the move. As a result, they already enjoy the synergetic advantages that a global network of bases can offer for

Lambert International Airport, Main Terminal, St. Louis, Missouri, 1955

Priory Chapel, St. Louis, Missouri, 1962

the electronic distribution and redistribution of workload, while at the same time every overseas outpost has become a semi-autonomous satellite, like an asteroid in space with a gravitational system of its own, always capable of attracting further work.

Hellmuth, Obata + Kassabaum, named in 1998 the biggest architectural practice in the world[2], is just such a firm, already immersed in what, even ten years ago, would have seemed like a science fiction existence. Founded in 1955 with a staff of two dozen in St. Louis, Missouri, at a time when stretched hand-made paper, wooden models, and fuzzy blueprints were the tools of architectural practice, HOK now has as many offices worldwide as it once had employees, and numbers its state-of-the-art CADD workstations by the hundred. Yet, although its long history stretches back to an era that now seems primitive, its current identity seems in no way constrained by it. Nor does it seem to be constrained by the memory of any particular building designed in its offices (though many are admired), nor by any one particular building type (although the firm has expertise in many). This is because the technological and market changes of recent years have diluted and romanticized the authority of tradition, so that what defines the identity of HOK today is something more elusive than a reputation for longevity or a memory of past critical success. In its place is something drawn from the fruitful contrast that now exists between the firm's image—epitomized by the venerable initials HOK and the continued presence of one of the firm's founding fathers in an active role—and the reality of the continuous changes that take place behind it.

Less noticeably in the firm's early years, but more certainly in the last decade when new technology and massive growth swept through the whole universe of architecture, HOK's image of

stability has acted as a kind of heraldic symbol behind which the firm has been able to undergo organizational transformations and embark upon new ventures and acquisitions that would have torn a less flexible organization apart. In the early 1990s, new offices were opened in Tokyo, Berlin, Mexico City, and Shanghai. The 1994 acquisition of CRS Architects added four U.S. offices and an advance planning service. In 1995, HOK acquired CDH of London, adding an office in Warsaw and leading to an HOK presence in Moscow and Prague. As a result of its alliance with Nortel and increasing design work for the telecommunications leader, HOK acquired Urbana Architects of Toronto in 1997 and began to establish an office there. A project office has also since opened in Ottawa.

Combine these major events with a background scattering of a few other business acquisitions and transitions, and then add to them the emergence of a number of new groups within the firm—one

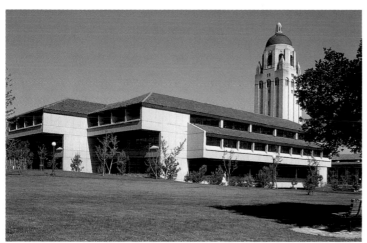

Stanford University Library, Stanford, California, 1965

Dallas/Fort Worth International Airport, Dallas, Texas, 1974

of which, HOK Sport, has grown since 1983 to be responsible for 15 percent of the firm's work—and the advantages of tradition become clear. In the 1990s, HOK enthusiastically enlarged and diversified itself. From outside, where observers saw only the most obvious end product of these changes—the firm's steady increase in size—the whole phenomenon may have been misunderstood by some. From inside it drew forth, among other things, the best explanation of the nature of HOK ever offered: the often quoted declaration by its president and chief executive that "HOK is not a static organization, it is a work in progress."[3]

Progress is indeed what ties HOK irrevocably to the future and enables it to deal realistically with its own past. For while the current balance of shareholders may stabilize by the year 2000, change will clearly not end there. It is far more likely that HOK will continue to be a work that progresses, making and remaking itself as the circumstances governing the practice of architecture evolve, and all the while responding by growing and expanding to keep pace with greater changes in the world at large. To which end, it might be noted that the firm is already among the largest purchasers of airline tickets in St. Louis, a city that is host to more than 15 *Fortune* 500 company headquarters.

How then did this giant of architecture come into existence? HOK was the outcome of the 1955 break-up of the St. Louis firm of Hellmuth, Yamasaki and Leinweber, which had recently completed the design of Lambert International Airport, an elegant concrete vaulted structure by the firm's design partner Minoru Yamasaki that serves the city to this day. The break-up occurred because, at the end of the Lambert project, a group of HYL architects, including senior partner George Hellmuth and designer Gyo Obata, decided to establish a new partnership with St. Louis architect George Kassabaum. The leaders of this group

were all graduates of the School of Architecture at Washington University in St. Louis and it was because of this local connection that they chose to remain in the St. Louis area.

The new firm grew steadily in the 1960s, attracting professional and popular respect for the design of its functional modern educational buildings. It also attracted particular attention through two small but highly unusual concrete structures designed by Obata himself: the St. Louis Benedictine Chapel, and the city's planetarium (now the St. Louis Science Center), which stands in the park landscaped for the 1904 St. Louis World's Fair.

Metropolitan Square, St. Louis, Missouri, 1989

National Air and Space Museum, Washington, D.C., 1976

Today, both these buildings are objects of pilgrimage by architects and students from all over the world, as are the same architect's 630,000-square-foot Smithsonian Air and Space Museum (completed in 1976 and still one of the most popular museums in the world with over eight million visitors a year); his 139,880-square-foot Reorganized Church of Jesus Christ of Latter Day Saints Temple in Independence, Missouri (completed in 1993); his 161,400-square-foot Florida Aquarium in Tampa (completed in 1995 in association with EHDD and Joseph Wetzel & Associates); and the 107,600-square-foot Tokyo Telecom building in Japan (completed in 1997 and designed with Nissoken Architects and Engineers).

In all these designs there is embodied evidence not only of a great gift, but also of a clarity of thought and lucidity of organization that is not confined to the architect himself. It is reflected in other less well-known projects across the firm as well as in HOK's management and administrative structure, which is now responsible for a huge spread of projects, both typologically and geographically. HOK's design integrity could not be maintained without the pre-existence of the culture of excellence nurtured for so many years by the firm's mentor.

In the decades since its foundation, HOK has undertaken projects in greater numbers, on a larger and more complicated scale, using more and more advanced technology, without ever losing its spark of originality and freshness of approach. The extent to which the firm's architecture is not identified with a house style derives as much from this talisman as it does from all the other strands of its complex identity. Because HOK started out in business with only two dozen employees and a single office in the American Midwest in 1955, it would hardly be surprising if by now its worldwide presence and its 2,000-plus employees represented

something very different. Although the firm's corporate offices are located in a downtown St. Louis HOK-designed office tower completed in 1989, the firm's geographical expansion from this Midwestern city began nearly 30 years ago, ten years after its foundation, when HOK was commissioned to design a new library for Stanford University in California. The supervision of that project opened up the opportunity to found an office in San Francisco to serve the West Coast and, once planted there, HOK grew to include offices in Los Angeles and Seattle.

Following that first expansionary move, the firm also opened offices in several other cities in response to major commissions. Washington, D.C., followed the Smithsonian Air and Space Museum; Dallas followed the construction of Dallas/Fort Worth International Airport; Tampa followed the Burger King headquarters in Miami and the even bigger Tampa Convention Center. Kansas City (among HOK's largest) is the headquarters of the brilliantly successful HOK Sports Facilities Group. In the mid 1980s and in the 1990s, the firm opened its first overseas office in Hong Kong, followed by London, Tokyo, Berlin, Mexico City, Warsaw, Moscow, Prague, and Toronto, reflecting major advances into Asia, Eastern Europe, and Canada.

Tampa Convention Center, Tampa, Florida, 1990

Oriole Park at Camden Yards, Baltimore, Maryland, 1992

Another part of the secret of HOK's eternal youthfulness of approach can be found in the related management structure of all its offices, large and small. Each is headed by a management committee composed of a director of design, a managing principal, a marketing principal, and market sector leaders. This in itself is a function of the growth-induced geometry of the firm's administrative organization, for within every office is a functioning replica of the separation of powers originally shared by George Hellmuth, Gyo Obata, and George Kassabaum nearly 50 years ago. This pattern has been a key feature of the firm's organization, which in the late 1980s transitioned to four key leaders. It can be seen at the level of individual office space planning—all HOK offices are open-plan to facilitate communication between staff—just as it can be detected in the composition of the five-member executive committee of the firm's board of directors. This committee oversees the four core competency boards representing the firmwide functions of design, management, marketing, and service delivery.

Another key element in HOK's structural flexibility is its approach to the task of recruitment over the years. Clearly any organization of such a size must lose a proportion of its staff every year and HOK estimates that natural attrition accounts for 13 to 15 percent annually. Depending on market conditions, this number or more are replaced, a process that is managed so skillfully that the firm is able to retain a capacity for freshness of approach in the face of the notion that growth breeds conformity.

Like most other large U.S. design firms, HOK has endeavored to decentralize its decision-making powers as a response to distant operations so that initiative can be encouraged and rewarded at the furthest outposts of the organization. This capacity for the simultaneous deployment of distant decision-making coupled with access to group resources is something that can be clearly seen in HOK's predesign programming operations. The firm also makes considerable efforts to promote potential projects. In the case of the Florida Aquarium, for example, the Tampa office supported the local drive to fund the construction of the building for two years before the local funding consortium was finally able to issue a contract. During that period, HOK put in 1,500 hours of what the firm calls "homework."

Beyond HOK's geographical expansion, its distinctive management structure, its concern for recruitment, its decentralization of decision-making, and its capacity to support precontract research and promotional "homework" lies the firm's most advanced organizational feature: the informal mobilization of talent into "Focus Groups." HOK's Focus Groups are widely accessible teams of individuals whose expertise and experience leads them to seek opportunities in high-growth and emerging markets. The phenomenally successful Sports Facilities Group, ranked by *The Sporting News* as among the 100 most powerful

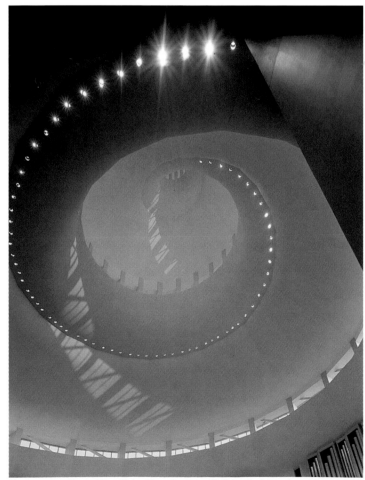

The Reorganized Church of Jesus Christ of Latter Day Saints World Temple, Independence, Missouri, 1993

The Florida Aquarium, Tampa, Florida, 1995

forces in the U.S. sports world, is HOK's most successful Focus Group and the only one that is completely contained in a single office. Groups for aviation, justice, health care, and entertainment (Studio E) have key representatives in New York, San Francisco, and other offices as well as in St. Louis.

Another distinct group was created in the wake of HOK's acquisition of CRS, a firm that had developed advance planning techniques for facilities. HOK integrated this service into HOK Consulting, a highly successful predesign programming offering for clients now responsible for nearly 10 percent of the firm's fee income. This group addresses growth predictions, rapidly changing client requirements, demand for flexible floorspace, short periods of occupancy, and planned exit strategies—all aspects of the architecture of the future that are already present within HOK today.

Providing a closely related service is HOK Interiors, a firmwide group of more than 150 interior designers and space planners. With the workplace increasingly transformed by new technologies and corporate change, new design strategies are needed for effective and flexible work spaces. HOK Planning takes on the macro view, by master planning whole regions and communities, as well as campuses and resorts. HOK Engineering provides services in structural, mechanical, and electrical engineering, as well as plumbing, fire protection, telecommunications, and security systems. Another specialized service is HOK Graphics, which plans and designs publications, signage, exhibits, and display environments as part of a client's overall visual identity program.

If it is possible to compare architectural firms with airlines, then the advantages gained by those architectural firms that have already succeeded in becoming global players are similar to those enjoyed by the first carriers to invest in wide-body jets. Their foresight made them more efficient than their narrow-body competitors, and gave them marketing advantages and economies of scale impossible to achieve by any other means.

Something similar has been achieved by HOK over the last 30 years of expansion. From the continued sparkling success of HOK Sport in the firm's domestic market and beyond, to the growing importance of the firm's retail and commercial work in Germany, the Czech Republic, Russia, and South America, there are now innumerable departure points for HOK into the 21st century. The priceless fruit of the firm's successful diversification in the past is that no single activity needs to provide the full impetus to ensure continued growth. In the years ahead it will be the task of HOK's leadership to make space for the exercise of firmwide talent and, through a period of tremendous change, that is something it has never failed to do.

Notes
1   *World Architecture* fifth annual survey of the top 500 architectural firms. *World Architecture* (no. 62, December 1997–January 1998).
2   Ibid., pp. 130–131.
3   Ibid., pp. 130–131.

Martin Pawley is an architectural writer and critic who contributes regularly to The Architects' Journal, *the Munich on-line magazine* Telepolis, World Architecture *(which he edited until his retirement in 1996), and the* Berliner Zeitung.

Recent books by Martin Pawley include Theory and Design in the Second Machine Age; Buckminster Fuller; Eva Jiricna: Design in Exile; *and* Future Systems: The Story of Tomorrow. *His most recent book,* Terminal Architecture, *is published by Reaktion Books, London.*

Tokyo Telecom Center, Tokyo, Japan, 1996

Nortel Brampton Centre, Brampton, Ontario, Canada, 1997

Mixed Use and Hospitality

Four Seasons Hotel, Shanghai, China

The Galleria

Design/Completion 1970/1986
Houston, Texas, U.S.A.
Gerald D. Hines Interests
4,000,000 square feet
Reinforced concrete structure with structural steel
Precast concrete panels, natural stone

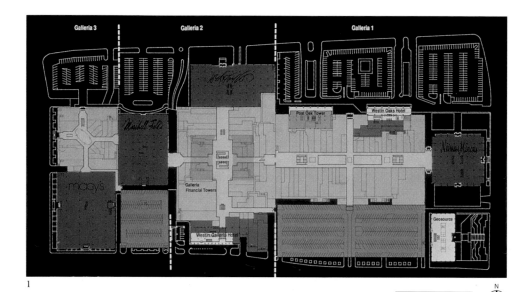

1

2

Inspired by European tradition, the Galleria combines the best in retail, hotel, entertainment, and office facilities in a carefully planned and interconnected complex.

Completed in three phases, the Galleria includes 1,873,000 square feet of retail space, including Neiman Marcus, Lord & Taylor, Marshall Field's, and Macy's; two hotels with convention facilities; four office towers ranging from 7 to 25 stories; an indoor ice-skating rink; and parking for 11,000 cars. A skylit pedestrian street provides physical and visual links to the buildings.

Flexibility and unity are major reasons for the Galleria's long-term success. A simple linear plan allows for easy expansion. The use of basic materials, combined with the limited palette of linear forms, builds a consistency that has been maintained through the many Galleria additions.

The Galleria was one of the first shopping malls to incorporate mixed uses. Over the years it has captured the public's imagination and maintained its attraction to local, national, and international customers.

3

1   Site plan
2   Exterior view of first anchor store
3   Indoor ice-skating rink
4   Atrium view from hotel guestrooms

Passenger Terminal Amsterdam

Design/Completion 1997/2000
Amsterdam, The Netherlands
Amsterdam Port Authority
350,000 square feet
Concrete and steel structure
Glass, steel, terracotta, brick

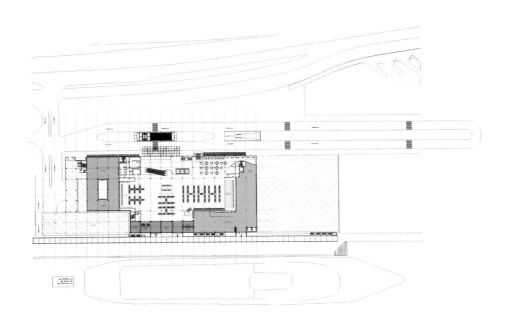

1

The Passenger Terminal Amsterdam establishes a 21st century benchmark for European transportation interchanges. It is the first completed building in the regeneration master plan co-authored by HOK and the City of Amsterdam for the revitalization of the city's Eastern Docks—a strategic catalyst for urban vitality and renewal.

The waveform arc of glass forms a gateway to Amsterdam that frames a view of the city skyline. The transparency of the building maintains constant visual contact with the ship. Cobalt blue tiling on all vertical circulation elements helps wayfinding while the heavy timber beams are a reminder of Amsterdam's shipbuilding tradition.

2

3

1 Site plan
2 Waveform arc of glass forms a gateway to
  Amsterdam
3 Carpark entrance at dusk
4 Viewing platform boomerang detail
5 Arrivals hall looking west
6 Level two looking south
Following page:
  Entrance hall looking east

Arena Central

Design/Completion 1997/2002
Birmingham, England, U.K.
Hampton Trust
2,300,000 square feet
Steel frame
Granite, limestone, brick, glass and metal curtain wall

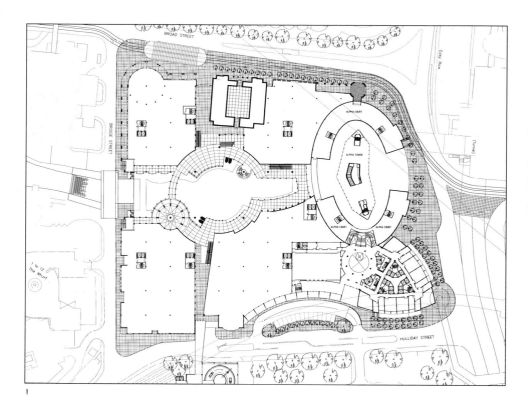

Re-integrating the site with the city core's urban fabric was the major challenge for this high-end mixed-use facility. A comprehensive understanding of the site's history, context, and current condition, as well as Birmingham's architecture helped formulate the redevelopment strategy.

With a 450-bed four-star hotel, high-quality office and residential components, and an array of entertainment and leisure facilities, Arena Central revitalizes the area by creating a lively and dynamic public space and linking major nodal points within Birmingham.

1   Site plan
2   Computer-enhanced exterior view
3   Rendering of atrium

Abu Dhabi Trade Center

Design/Completion 1996/2001
Abu Dhabi, United Arab Emirates
3,010,000 square feet
Cast-in-place concrete structure with post-tensioned girders and structural steel trusses
Granite; limestone; polished, precast, high thermal performance aluminum and glass curtain wall

1

The integration of complementary yet distinct urban activities guided the design of this mixed-use center in Abu Dhabi. Patrons will work, shop, dine, and enjoy leisure activities within a single complex offering superior residential and hotel accommodation.

Each of the center's dual identities is in keeping with its surroundings. The urban side facing the city center establishes a formal entry to the development. The other side, facing the waters of the Arabian Gulf, accommodates informal beach and leisure activities.

Twin 20-story office towers signal the entry to the complex and provide a visual marker amid the surrounding 10- and 12-story developments. The hotel component is a 184-room luxury addition to the existing Beach Hotel. Thirteen floors above the retail mall, it affords sweeping views over the Arabian Gulf.

2

3

1   Site plan
2   Street level view
3   Aerial view of model
4   Atrium
5   Hotel facade facing Arabian Gulf

4

5

St. George Intermodal Terminal

Design/Completion 1999/2004
Staten Island, New York, New York, U.S.A.
New York Economic Development Corporation
190,000 square feet
Steel frame
Aluminum and glass curtain wall, existing brick, corrugated metal panel,
insulated metal panel, steel and aluminum canopies

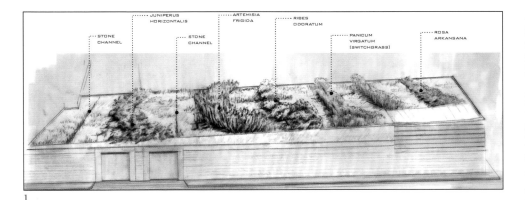

1

Among the renovation project's primary goals was the enhancement of the commuter experience while realizing the station's potential as the gateway to Staten Island. The station will be the first LEED™ (Leadership in Energy and Environmental Design)–certified intermodal transportation center in the U.S. Sustainable design initiatives include a living roof, photovoltaics, water recycling, and recycled building materials.

Originally built to accommodate bus, car, and rail connections to the terminal and process commuters to ferries, the existing terminal design gave little attention to the site's aesthetic potential or impact on the adjacent waterfront development.

The new design incorporates more light and air, harbor and Manhattan views, usable exterior spaces, seamless commuter connections, connections to neighboring sites, and new destination retail.

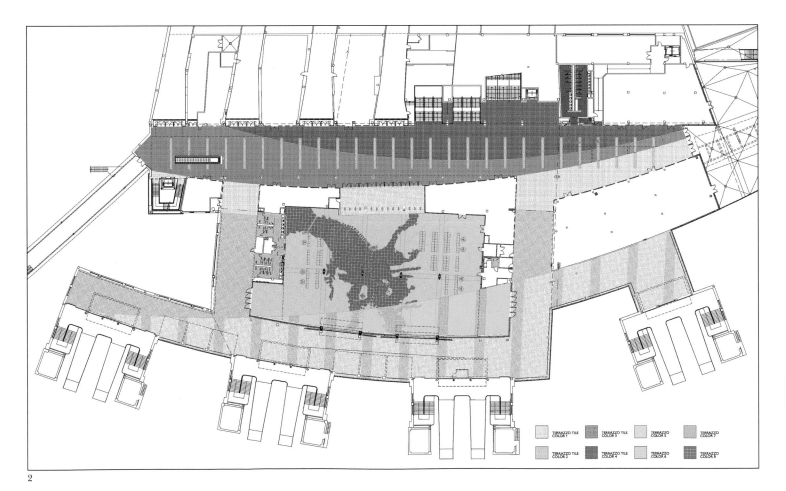

2

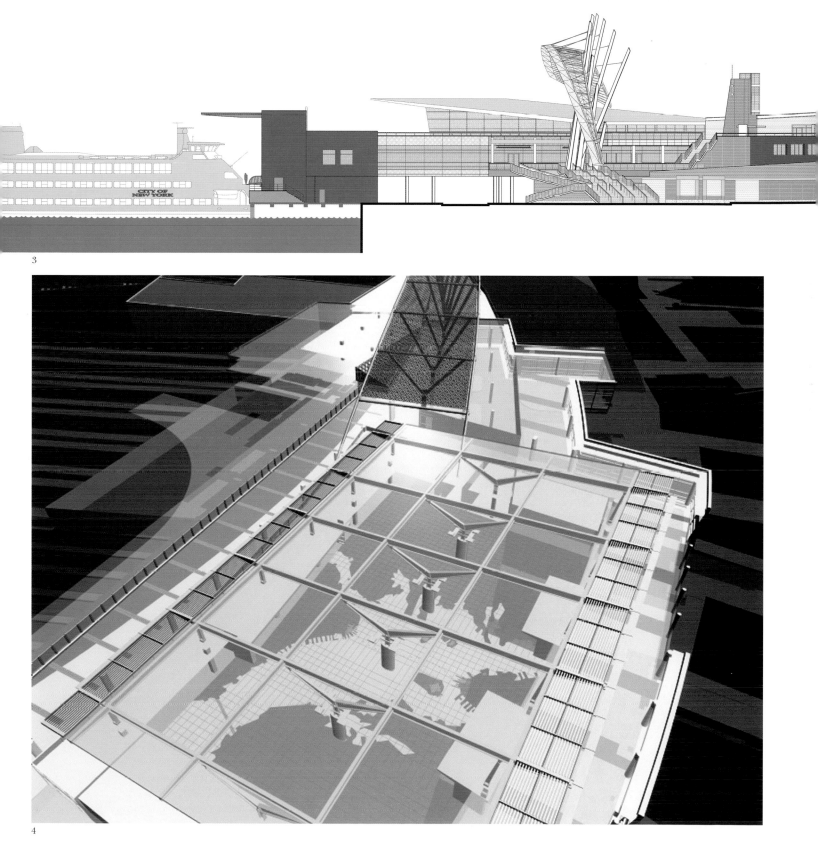

3

4

Moscow High-Speed Rail Terminal

Design/Completion 1997/2001
St. Petersburg, Russia
VSM Limited
1,500,000 square feet
Steel and concrete structure
Stucco, granite, metal panels
Associate architect: LenNIIproekt

1

The design for the Moscow High-Speed Rail Terminal creates a mixed-use complex integrating traditional urban design and civic planning principles with historic architectural contextualism to satisfy the needs of a contemporary development. The facility is next to the October Railway Station (circa 1851) in the center of historic St. Petersburg.

The development consists of six office buildings arranged around a glazed galleria with arcade shopping, a 360-room international hotel, a luxury serviced apartment tower, and a new rail terminal for a high-speed train linking St. Petersburg with Moscow. The building materials, details, and colors reflect the traditional architecture of eighteenth- and nineteenth-century St. Petersburg.

2

3

1   Aerial view
2   Central galleria
3   Interior perspective

Dortmund Mixed-Use Development

Design/Completion 2001/2005
Berlin, Germany
Sonae Imobiliária in conjunction with Sonae West, Stadt Dormund
and Deutsche Bahn
592,000 square feet
Concrete and steel structure
Precast concrete panels, timber louver panels, copper/metal
panels, glass

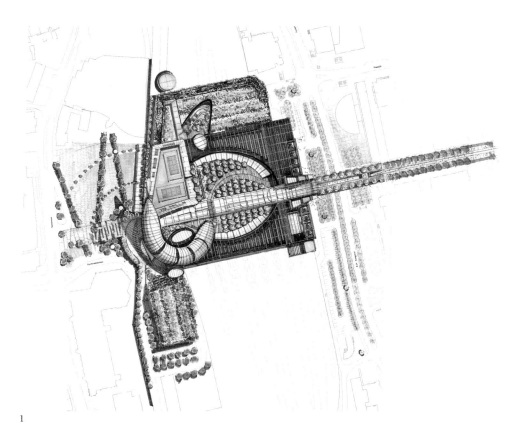

1

Dortmund Station is being redeveloped to provide improved transport facilities, retail and leisure, and a hotel. Arranged on a north-south axis, the center will link the isolated north and thriving south portions of Berlin and contribute to the cityscape.

Twelve new platforms will improve existing station facilities and provide platforms for the high-speed magnetic Metro Rapide. Above the platforms is 600,000 square feet of new commercial space arranged around a landscaped glazed gallery. Crowning the development is a 20-story spiral tower with a platform providing views of St. Katherine's Church along the retail gallery axis.

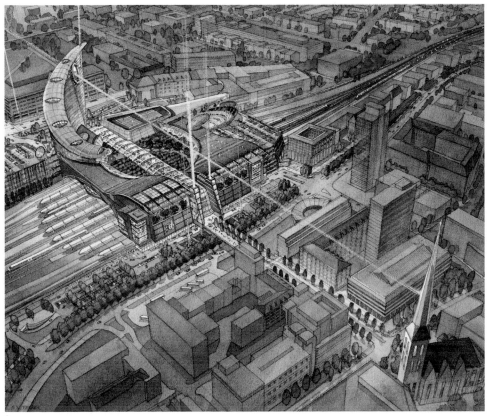

2

1   Roof garden rendering
2   The center links the south and north sides of Berlin

Mulia Hotel Senayan

Design/Completion 1996/1997
Jakarta, Indonesia
Mulia Group
1,250,000 square feet
Reinforced concrete structure
Aluccobond and glass for the tower; granite, stainless steel and glass
at the first three floors

1

Envisioned as a five-star hospitality property for the new millennium, the Mulia Hotel Senayan is remarkable both for its opulence and for the speed at which it was delivered: from conception to grand opening in just 10 months.

The 40-story hotel tower's timeless modern architecture is rendered in a contrasting pattern of aluminum and blue-green glass. An architectural crowning element establishes the hotel's contemporary identity while creating a distinctive addition to the Jakarta skyline. An elegant roof garden sits atop a rich stone building base that houses three stories of world-class public areas.

Inside, the hotel presents a forward-looking design concept, expressed through the open public areas and the 1,000 guestrooms and suites. Guests approach the hotel through an expansive porte-cochere, positioned on the second level to create a sense of enclosure from the surrounding city streets. The lobby and registration areas are characterized by distinctive contemporary furnishings and rich, subtle materials such as honey-colored movinguewood, black Portoro marble, and Mexican honey onyx.

1 View of front exterior
2 Plan of typical guestroom floor
3 Guestroom
4 Dining room

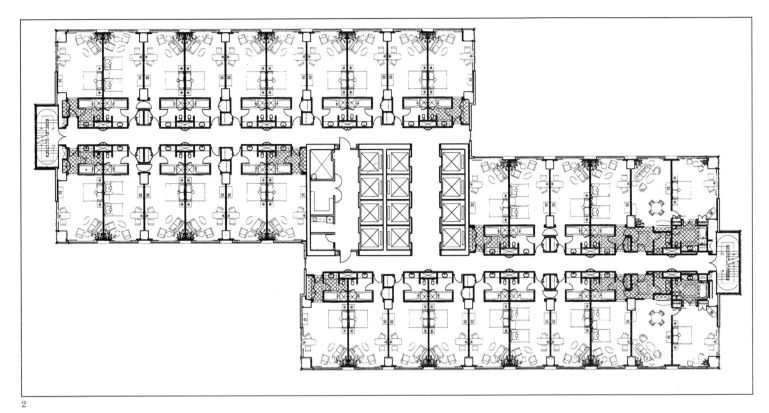

2

3

4

Sheraton Inn at Timika

Design/Completion 1992/1994
Irian Jaya, Indonesia
P.T. Freeport Indonesia
180,000 square feet
Concrete and steel structure
Local river stone, ironwood (*kayu besi*) from the site and surrounding area

1

2

Minimizing the impact of the guesthouse on the environment was of primary importance in the design of this remote resort at the edge of a tropical rain forest.

The main lodge of the Sheraton Inn at Timika rests on an expressed base of local river stone. This contrasts with the supporting stilts that elevate guestroom bungalows above the rain forest floor, preserving the fragile nature of the flora, fauna, and water table.

The main lodge houses the reception area, lobby, restaurant, meeting rooms, and fitness center. Interior lobby finishes feature a select palette of Indonesian woods, marble, and stone. Merbau, a wood found in Irian Jaya, was used for the floors and exterior trim. Doors and furniture are made from sunkai, a native wood from Sumatra. All furnishings and textiles were designed and manufactured in Indonesia.

1   Aerial view
2   Hotel entrance
3   Elevated bilevel walkways connect the bungalows
4   Lobby

3

4

5 Typical guestroom
6 Lobby
7 Main dining room
8 Exterior pavilion

5

6

7

30 Sheraton Inn at Timika Hellmuth, Obata + Kassabaum

Hellmuth, Obata + Kassabaum **Sheraton Inn at Timika** **31**

TABA Hotel

Design/Completion 2000/2004
Taba, Red Sea Coast, Republic of Egypt
TTDC (Taba Tourism Development Company)
370,273 square feet
Concrete structure
Local Egyptian stone, stucco, wood screens

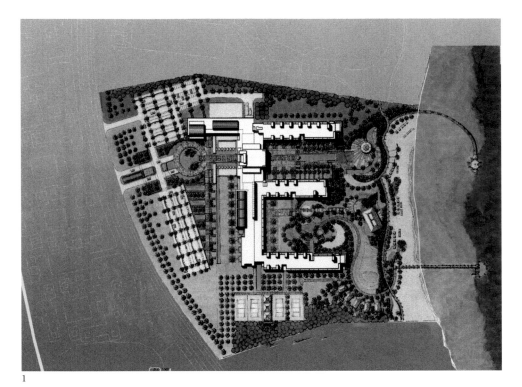

The TABA Hotel is a 250-room five-star resort and conference hotel on the coast of the Gulf of Aqaba.

The site offers beachfront access and unobstructed views to the Gulf of Aqaba. The design takes full advantage of the surrounding environment. Each room has a view of the sea as well as access to lush, landscaped courtyards and pools.

In addition to the hotel and conference facilities, the development features restaurants, a coffee shop, a ballroom, an auditorium, a business center, and a health club.

A variety of recreational activities allows guests to enjoy the Gulf's clear warm waters and abundant coral and marine life.

1

2

3

4

Sheraton Grand Hotel

Design/Completion 1999/2001
Sacramento, California, U.S.A.
David S. Taylor Interest, Inc., Keystone Development, Lankford &
Associates, Tynan Group, Inc., Vanir Construction Management
392,000 square feet
Concrete structure
Limestone base, GFRC, metal, glass

The Sheraton Grand Hotel provides a significant addition to the eastern end of downtown Sacramento in the area encompassing the Capitol complex and convention center.

The hotel provides 500 guestrooms in a 26-story tower adjacent to the 1923 Public Market Building designed by American architect Julia Morgan. This Public Market was renovated and adaptively reused as the heart of the hotel complex.

Other significant features include the 11,000-square-foot ballroom, 6,500 square feet of meeting rooms, upscale restaurant and bar facilities, convenient access to the "K" Street Mall and Convention Center, and nearby sidewalk shops.

1   Renovated 1923 Public Market Building serves as
    the entry to the new hotel
2   Lounge
3   New 26-story tower
4   Restaurant

Retail and Entertainment

MaiaShopping, Oporto, Portugal

Arrábida Shopping

Design/Completion 1993/1996
Villa Nova de Gia, Oporto, Portugal
Amorim-Imobiliaria
1,300,000 square feet
Poured-in-place concrete structure
Glass and steel truss roof structure, precast concrete panels with decorative
tile, curtain wall system with glass and metal panels

1

With the site resting on a hilltop overlooking the historic Portuguese city of Oporto and the emerging new town of Villa Nova de Gia, an appropriate civic response was paramount in the design of Arrábida Shopping, a new regional shopping center.

The mixed-use center includes a two-level hypermarket, three levels of retail shops, and an office building. The third-level entertainment zone offers restaurants, cafes, a 26-screen cinema (Europe's largest), and balcony views of Oporto.

The colonnaded facade of the 200,000-square-foot hypermarket faces the city and river, establishing a formal and civic entry to the complex. A distinctive arched glass and steel truss roof structure—inspired by bridges spanning the Douro River—rises above the five-level center court.

2

1 Site plan
2 Night view of main entry
3 Interior view of second level

3

Galeria Mokotów

Design/Completion 1998/2000
Warsaw, Poland
GTC Galeria Sp.z o.o.
871,905 square feet
Concrete frame
Precast concrete and ceramic panels

1   First floor plan
2   Main entry at night
3   Main floor concierge
4   Central atrium

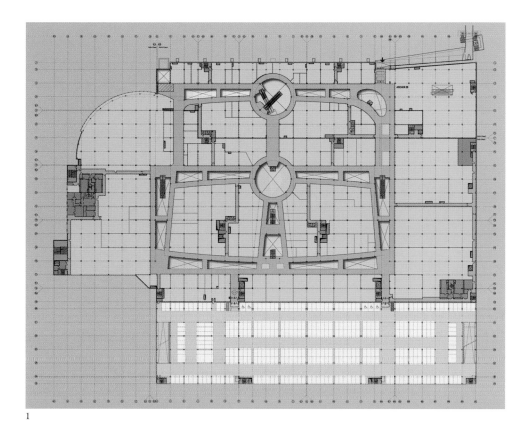

1

Designed to provide shopping and urban entertainment for the area between Warsaw's airport and city center, Galeria Mokotów contains approximately 800,000 square feet of retail space on two levels and an entertainment level above the retail complex.

The retail space is a typical shopping mall with several major anchors along the periphery and a large hypermarket on the ground floor. Pedestrian flow is organized around a generous interior street.

The center's focal point is a vertically organized atrium and circulation zone that brings visitors to all floors.

3

2

4

The Living World

Design/Completion 1984/1989
St. Louis, Missouri, U.S.A.
St. Louis Zoo
55,000 square feet
Steel and wood structure
Metal, glass, stone, brick, tile, wood

1

Teaching visitors about conserving the animal kingdom is the mission of the St. Louis Zoo's education center, The Living World.

The center comprises a cluster of four octagonal exhibit, theater, and multi-use spaces centered around a two-story rotunda. The 65-foot-high, 70-foot-wide rotunda is topped by a translucent skylight, creating a pavilion-like gathering space and circulation center at the building's heart. A wide balcony on the rotunda's upper level leads to two exhibition halls and serves as a zoo entrance.

The center's multifaceted, geometric design reflects the diversity of the animal kingdom and reduces the structure's apparent scale to harmonize with the natural surroundings.

2   3

1 Main entry
2 South elevation
3 Site plan
4 Exhibition hall
5 Interior rotunda
6 Main level

The Florida Aquarium

Design/Completion 1985/1995
Tampa, Florida, U.S.A.
The Florida Aquarium, Inc.
152,000 square feet
Reinforced concrete structure
Stucco and glass
Joint venture with EHDD (Esherick, Homsey, Dodge & Davis)
and Joseph A. Wetzel Associates, Inc., exhibit designers

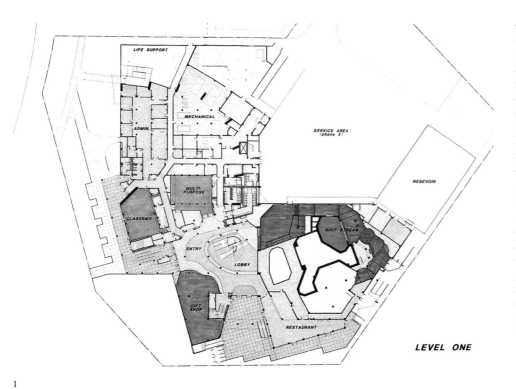

LEVEL ONE

1

LEVEL TWO

2

The purpose of the Florida Aquarium is to tell the story of Florida's diverse water habitats in an educational and entertaining way, while inspiring in visitors a sense of stewardship for the aquatic environment. The scheme provides enclosures for the marine animal and plant exhibits, as well as for free-flying birds, in a design that reflects the site's maritime surroundings.

The aquarium's prominent architectural element is a shell-shaped glass dome that covers the Florida Wetlands exhibit. The design of this space ensures that sufficient daylight is available to sustain native Florida habitats under near-natural conditions. Other aquarium spaces are designed to create an architectural flow from the entry, giving visitors a dramatic sense of rising up and winding through the exhibit layers of marine life, plants, and free-flying birds.

1 Level one plan
2 Level two plan
3 Outdoor terraces
4 Main entry

3

4

5 Florida Wetlands exhibit
6 Detail of glass dome
7 Interior of glass dome

5

6

Eisenhower Centre

Design/Completion 1999/2003
Madrid, Spain
Grupo Riofisa
753,474 square feet gross leasable area
Precast and in situ concrete frame
Clad in gabion stone walling, timber and precast concrete panels

1

The client expressed an expectation for a bold and imaginative leisure and entertainment center in Madrid.

The design creates an elliptical loop mall that provides frontage to 450,000 square feet of shops over two floors and provides a strong identity for the complex. Another 350,000 square feet of entertainment space, including a rooftop music court, is above the shopping levels.

A central plaza, an essential component of Spanish cities, is a fundamental component. Surrounded by a multi-level food and music court, as well as the access roads to the cinemas and family entertainment areas, the central plaza provides a reference space for leisure, recreation, and public assembly.
A reloadable fabric roof covers the plaza during inclement weather.

1   Aerial view with central plaza illuminated
2   Elevation showing central spine
3   Cross section

2

3

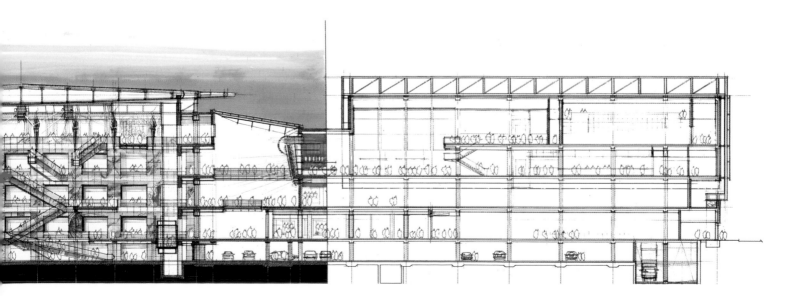

Long Beach Aquarium of the Pacific

Design/Completion 1994/1998
Long Beach, California, U.S.A.
City of Long Beach
145,000 square feet
Poured-in-place concrete and steel connected by long-span trusses
Exposed concrete, plaster
Joint venture with EHDD (Esherick, Homsey, Dodge & Davis)
and Joseph A. Wetzel Associates, Inc., exhibit designers

Drawing inspiration for both form and function from the nearby Pacific Ocean, the design of the Long Beach Aquarium features undulating curves echoing the movement of waves.

The lobby's three "eddies" contain preview tanks of major exhibits, sheltered by a trio of wave-like metal roofs. An extensive aluminum curtain wall punctuated with sea-green glass forms the entry and west wall.

Live aquatic exhibits from around the Pacific appear in natural settings; interactive exhibits represent the California coastal waters, the Bering Sea, Tropical Palao, and Indonesian and Japanese sea life.

To mitigate the threat posed by earthquakes on this Southern California marina site, the entire structure sits on a thick concrete mat foundation. Interior concrete tanks are designed to withstand earthquake-level lateral forces.

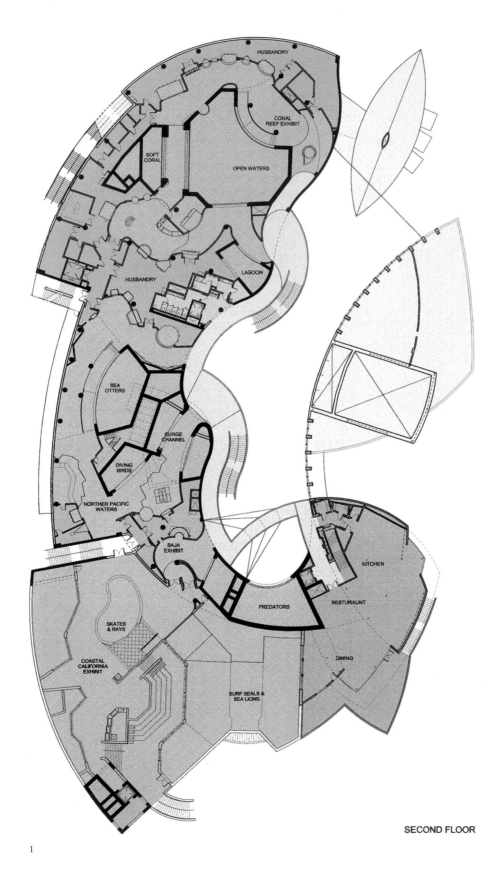

SECOND FLOOR

1

2

1   Floor plan
2   Aerial view
3   Waterside view
4   Exterior rendering

3

4

5 Main lobby
Opposite:
    Underwater exhibit

5

Guimaráes Shopping

Design/Completion 1993/1994
Guimaráes, Portugal
Sonae Imobiliaria
350,000 square feet
Precast concrete structure
Precast panels, granite, tile

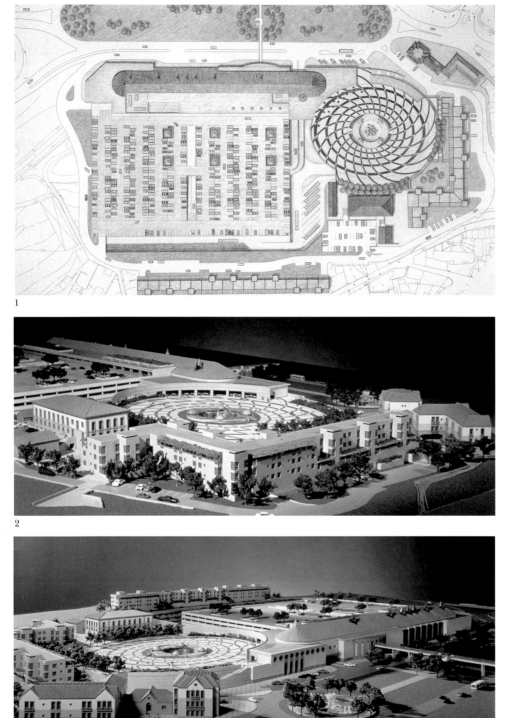

1

2

3

The key design objectives of Guimaráes Shopping, located in the town celebrated as Portugal's birthplace, were to reflect the region's history while serving as a vibrant transit and retail center.

In addition to the shopping center, an existing 500-year-old villa was restored and adapted for office use. Another historic building is designated for conversion to hotel use. Below the center's circular 3-acre civic plaza is a new regional bus station.

4

5

6

1   Site plan
2   Aerial view showing residential units
3   Main vehicular entry to retail complex
4   Facade detail
5   Food court
6   Shopping levels

O2 Centre

Design/Completion 1995/1998
London, England, U.K.
The Burford Group
350,000 square feet
Concrete frame
Brick, glass, precast panels with copper and glazed roof

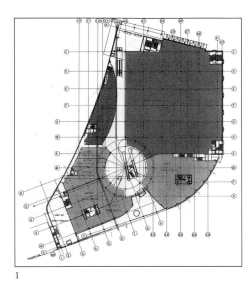

1

2

Located on Finchley Road, the O2 Centre provides a new retail, leisure, and entertainment destination in central London.

The development replaces the existing street frontage with a new 490-foot-long facade to Finchley Road. This new frontage provides direct access to restaurants and leisure activities.

Internally, all the restaurants and leisure spaces open to a central destination that offers an enclosed environment for pavement cafes and performance events within a richly landscaped piazza space.

The design maintains distinct separation among the entertainment, restaurant, leisure destination, and everyday shopping facilities.

3

4

1 First floor plan
2 Lower level of atrium
3 Landscaped piazza
4 Shopping area

Sports

Heinz Field, Pittsburgh, Pennsylvania, U.S.A.

Wembley Stadium

Design/Completion 1999/2005
London, England, U.K.
Wembley National Stadium Ltd.
90,000 seats
Steel on concrete base
Aluminum framed glazing, anodised aluminum panels, precast concrete panels, stainless steel mesh
Joint venture with World Stadium Team, HOK Sport + Venue + Event, and Foster and Partners

1

This extraordinary design for England's new National Soccer Stadium continues the "Venue of Legends" reputation of the original 1923 Wembley structure. The new Wembley Stadium design creates a digital-age, "fourth-generation stadium" responsive to the needs of many types of events.

Wembley's distinctive pitch is one of the finest in the world. The new roof will uphold that reputation and contain retractable elements.

The stadium is designed primarily for soccer, but also will accommodate rugby, athletics meetings, and major entertainment events.

2

1 Wembley was designed to be flexible and accommodate a variety of events
2 The new stadium will be located in the London Borough of Brent with convenient access to transportation
3 A spectacular arch was designed to mark the entry of the stadium and serve as a dramatic landmark across the city
4 The new seating bowl design improves upon the previous stadium

3

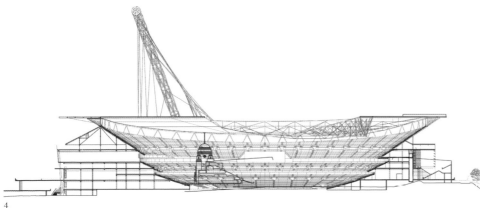

4

Gaylord Entertainment Center

Design/Completion 1993/1996
Nashville, Tennessee, U.S.A.
Metropolitan Government of Nashville and Davidson County
1 million square feet; 19,000 (basketball), 18,500 (hockey), 20,000 concert seats
Steel and concrete structure
Spread footings, cast-in-place concrete retaining walls, columns, beams, rakers, precast seating treads and deck, insulation and PVC roofing, architectural precast metal panel exterior skin with tinted glazing

1 Located in the heart of downtown Nashville, Gaylord Entertainment Center has served as a catalyst for urban development
2 Transparent concourse walls create a connection between events inside the center and the surrounding downtown area
3 Dramatic lighting accentuates the nighttime appearance of Gaylord Entertainment Center
4 Restaurants and bars throughout the center accommodate patrons before and after shows

The exuberance and vitality of musical performance inspired the design for Gaylord Entertainment Center.

The roof resembles a music box lid lifted slightly to let sound escape. The major walls of the concourse are transparent, revealing sweeping stair elements that offer a glimpse of the inner works of a performance. Catwalks and lighting grids at the main entry complete the "stage" and encourage spectators to become part of the performance.

A 22-story glass and steel broadcast tower links the arena to the rich musical heritage of Nashville by creating an icon symbolic of the radio broadcasts from the Grand Ole Opry.

1

2

3

4

Brisbane Football Stadium at Lang Park

Design/Completion 2000/2003
Brisbane, Australia
Queensland State Government
706,651 square feet; 52,500 seats
In situ concrete and steel form with precast concrete floor planks, structural steel trussed roof
Curtain wall glazing, timber screen sunshading, metal mesh screens, precast concrete and pre-finished CFC facades

1

The Brisbane Football Stadium at Lang Park is Australia's first modern dedicated rectangular pitch stadium. The design reflects Queensland's subtropical climate and outdoor lifestyle.

The seating bowl maximizes cross ventilation of the seating area and pitch. Open corners in the upper tier circulate local breezes around the seats. The flattened roof encloses noise and ensures unrestricted views from residential areas.

Recycled timber is used for solar screens fronting the large glazed areas that enclose the restaurant and dining sections. These screens create transition zones between the external environment and building facade and help minimize heat gain from solar radiation.

2

1 Open air terraces and viewing galleries provide a modern interpretation of traditional Australian stadium features
2 The stadium is the first modern dedicated rectangular pitch stadium in Australia
3 The Brisbane Football Stadium at Lang Park has been designed to complement and blend into the surrounding area
4 The stadium is set in the heart of a residential area on the edge of the city's CBD

3

4

Pacific Bell Park

Design/Completion 1995/2000
San Francisco, California, U.S.A.
San Francisco Giants
1 million square feet
Cast-in-place concrete superstructure and structural steel
Thin brick integral with precast concrete panel plus exposed architectural
precast concrete, exposed and painted metal panel detail

Pacific Bell Park offers baseball fans a sporting venue unparalleled in spectator amenities, accessibility, and panoramic beauty.

The ballpark, which turns its back on the strong westerly winds, borders China Basin in the northeast section of the city. The red brick and precast concrete exterior responds to the architecture of the surrounding neighborhood.

From inside the stadium, fans enjoy spectacular views of the Bay Bridge and the San Francisco skyline. Each at-bat presents another opportunity to see a home run splash into the Bay. A waterfront promenade beyond the outfield offers the public a glimpse into the ballpark.

1   The ballpark is unparalleled in spectator amenities, accessibility, and panoramic beauty
2   Baseball themes continue throughout the ballpark's bars and concession areas
3   A sculpture of legendary Giants ballplayer Willie Mays greets visitors to the ballpark
4   A public promenade along the waterfront from right field to center field offers the public a free glimpse into the ballpark

1

2

3

4

Millennium Stadium

Design/Completion 1995/1999
Cardiff, Wales, U.K.
Millennium Stadium, Ltd.
860,000 square feet; 75,000 seats
Concrete and steel truss frame
Kal-zip aluminum standing system roof,
aluminum curtain walling and glazing system

Millennium Stadium is designed to catalyze the regeneration of Cardiff's city center.

The acoustically insulated retractable roof is the first in the U.K. and one of the largest of its type in the world. The roof enables all types of sports, leisure, and cultural events to take place year-round. Seating is flexible for different uses.

The stadium interior has a three-tiered profile. The middle tier provides club and corporate seating, with private hospitality boxes at the rear.

The stadium's six levels include concessions ranging from fast food to reserved table restaurants, merchandise franchises and retail outlets, a museum of sport, and childcare facilities.

1   Total integration with the surrounding urban precinct is a feature of this famous venue, allowing easy pedestrian links with existing public transport terminals
2   The stadium's retractable roof provides 75,000 seats with total weather protection
3   The Millennium Stadium is located on the waterfront in Cardiff city center
4   The stadium offers unrivaled facilities for spectators, and is adjacent to a variety of retail and leisure plaza developments

1

Nanjing Olympic Sports Centre

Design/Completion 2001/2005
Nanjing, China
Jiangsu State-Owned Assets Operation (Holding) Co., Ltd.
200 acres; 60,000-seat stadium, 11,000-seat arena
Concrete frame with steel roof
Glass and metal panels

The Nanjing Olympic Sports Centre is designed to create a "People's Place" for the citizens of Nanjing. The Centre includes a stadium, sports arena, aquatic center, baseball and softball parks, and a tennis center.

The stadium's hyperbolic roof structure is a landmark feature that provides cover for every seat. The roof's lightweight, transparent polycarbonate material reduces shadows over the field and lends an open feeling.

The elliptical-shaped arena allows for easy changeover for various events. The lower seating bowl has both fixed and retractable seating.

The aquatic center is a low, discreet building that adopts a self-consciously styled "sea animal" form.

1

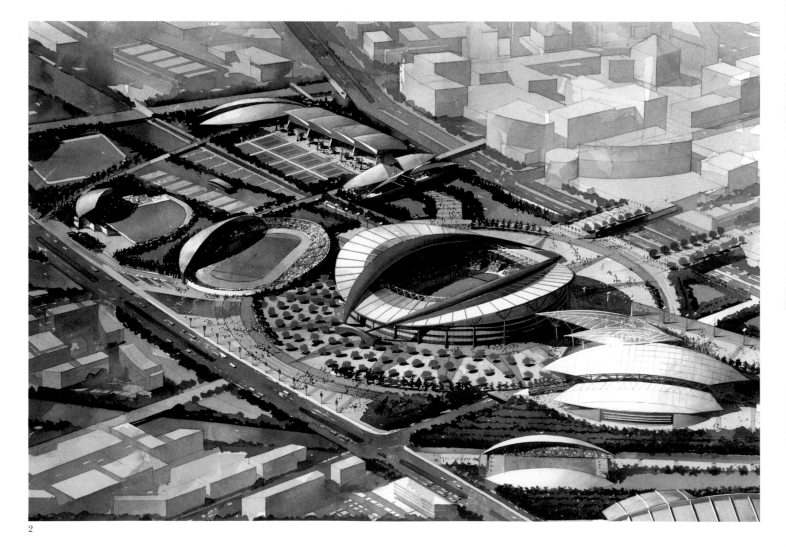

2

3

1   The main stadium was designed as a signature
    attraction for the City of Nanjing
2   Situated on a riverfront, the center includes separate
    facilities for a wide variety of sporting events
3   The Nanjing Olympic Sports Precinct forms the
    centerpiece of a new downtown development

Philips Arena

Design/Completion 1996/1999
Atlanta, Georgia, U.S.A.
Atlanta-Fulton County Recreation Authority
680,000 square feet; 20,000 (basketball), 18,750 (hockey) seats
Cast-in-place concrete, exposed steel at main concourse and roof
Steel, granite, glass

1

2

Philips Arena's interior is intimate and innovative. Foregoing the traditional placement of suites in a single row around the arena, the design places an entire quadrant of suites on one side of the court. This allows the majority of the seats to be located in the lowest seating level and pushes upper seating levels closer to the action. A variable-rise seating system at each end raises and retracts to accommodate different events.

The roof is made up of four planes that from above resemble playing cards scattered across a table. Each roof appears both razor-sharp and curved, creating a terraced effect.

3

1 The arena is the dynamic keystone of a 25-acre development in downtown Atlanta
2 Philips is the first arena to diverge from the traditional seating bowl, with its 83 luxury suites stacked on one side
3 The signature aluminum-clad ATLANTA entrance provides not only a unique sculptural element to the arena but also an integral structural component to support the roof
4 Philips Arena offers a wide variety of seating and dining options

4

New Stadium for Arsenal Football Club

Design/Completion 1999/2003
London, England, U.K.
Arsenal Football Club
60,000 seats
Reinforced concrete frame with steel and precast concrete rakers holding up the terracing, roof of exposed tubular steel frame with metal clad underside
Entry level—exposed concrete, Reglit® glazing and frameless glazing at VIP entries; Upper levels—inclined double-glazed curtain walling and exposed stainless stair mesh over concrete cores

The new Arsenal Stadium features an undulating roof canopy suspended in an ellipse above the stands. The inverse roof structure provides for complete enclosure and uninterrupted views of the arena.

The facility will seat 60,000 people, including 29,000 in the lower tier and 24,000 in the upper tier. Club levels will accommodate 7,000 visitors. The stadium includes the Arsenal Museum and Shop and several restaurants and bars.

Rainwater will be collected and stored for reuse in irrigation, washdown, and toilet flushing. Passive ventilation will minimize the use of air conditioning. Integration of natural and artificial lighting will maximize energy and cost-efficiency.

1

2

1 The urban site required extensive consultation with resident groups and heritage officers to produce a highly technical solution that fit architectural merit requirements
2 This complex is the most significant development at Highbury since the 1930s
3 This stand provides over 12,000 seats with a level of hospitality and servicing rarely seen
4 A terminal was set up in the Arsenal Shop where customers could check the view from their seats before they purchased

3

4

Stadium Australia

Design/Completion 1996/1999
Sydney, Australia
Stadium Australia Management Ltd.
Seating capacity (during Olympics) 110,000; (post-Olympics) 80,000
Concrete with graded polycarbonate roof on steel truss frame
Metal cladding, glazed panels
Stadium Australia was designed by an HOK Sport + Venue + Event
joint venture – Bligh Lobb Sports Architecture

1

Stadium Australia's roof is a hyperbolic paraboloid, offering protection to twice the number of spectators as compared to cantilevered roof stadiums. This roof shape also allows rainwater to be siphoned off into tanks to irrigate the pitch. The roof is supported by the seating structure and two long trusses.

The facility's retractable seating tiers allow it to be converted for various sports, concerts, exhibitions, and public gatherings.

Circulation routes for spectators, athletes, and services personnel never cross, providing optimum security and convenience.

2

1 The flexible design incorporates movable tiers to allow optimum sightlines for different events
2 The roof's translucent cover was designed to even out contrasts in lighting and prevent shadows, creating a better viewing experience for both live and television audiences
3 The stadium was designed to accommodate an additional 30,000 spectators during the Olympics
4 Stadium Australia serves as Australia's first world-class stadium and is the largest Olympic stadium in the history of the modern Olympic Games

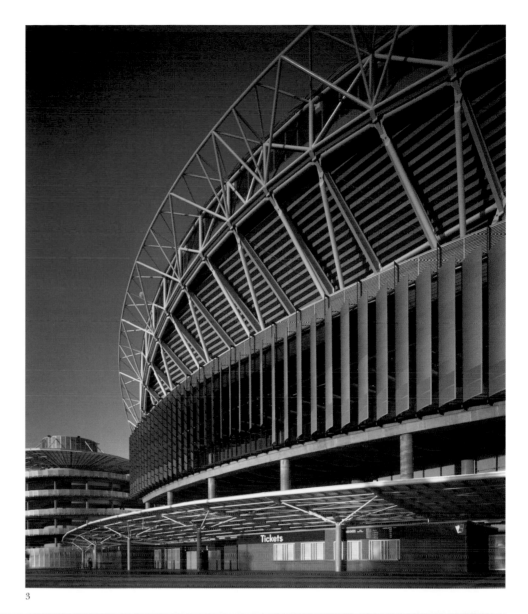

3

4

5   The stadium's roof is supported by the seating structure and 970-foot-long trusses measuring more than half the span of Sydney's Harbour Bridge

6   Selective use of finishes, materials, and lighting create unique and dramatic interior spaces

5

6

Venues

Anaheim Convention Center Expansion, Anaheim, California, U.S.A.

George R. Moscone Convention Center
(Moscone Center)

Design/Completion 1977/1981
San Francisco, California, U.S.A.
City of San Francisco
640,000 square feet (12-acre site)
Post-tension concrete structure
Concrete, glass
Associate architect: Jack Young & Associates

1   Night view of above-ground entrance lobby
2   The center was designed to be a predominantly
    underground facility for conventions, meetings,
    and exhibits

Moscone Center was the first project to start construction within downtown San Francisco's controversial Yerba Buena Center Redevelopment Area. The convention center was built primarily underground to satisfy the City's voter mandate that it not be visible above grade.

Eight pairs of post-tensioned concrete arches anchored to a massive concrete mat foundation support a 275,000-square-foot exhibit hall. The arch frame design allows for column-free exhibit space, creating a sense of openness and increasing the hall's flexibility. The center includes a 30,000-square-foot ballroom that holds up to 4,000 people.

A skylit above-ground entrance lobby connects the exhibit hall with meeting rooms and related facilities.

1

2

Tampa Convention Center

Design/Completion 1986/1990
Tampa, Florida, U.S.A.
City of Tampa
677,000 square feet
Steel frame
Precast concrete, glass
Associate architect: Ranon & Partners

A desire to create an environment that is unique to Florida guided the design of the Tampa Convention Center. The center occupies 13 acres of shoreline nestled at the mouth of the Hillsborough River and offering scenic views of the Seddon Channel and Tampa Bay.

Natural light pours into the 95-foot tall building from clerestory windows, creating an open, airy feeling that belies its large scale. Exterior colors are reminiscent of a coquina shell's pink, beige, and blue tones. Interior colors feature shades of blue, coral, and green accented with touches of lightly-tinted woodwork.

Inside the center on street level are 18 meeting rooms that can be configured to serve 30 to 800 people, and 36,000 square feet of ballroom space. On the second level is a 200,000-square-foot exhibit hall that can host up to 17,000 people.

1 Pedestrian plaza with stairs to exhibit hall
2 View of main entry from across the bay

America's Center Expansion and Edward Jones Dome

Design/Completion 1987/1995
St. Louis, Missouri, U.S.A.
City of St. Louis

America's Center
414,000 square feet
Steel frame
Brick with limestone and metal trim and floral ornamentation

Edward Jones Dome
1,700,000 square feet (70,000 seats)
Poured-in-place concrete beams with concrete floors, steel trusses for the roof structure
Brick, terracotta panels, cast stone treatments

The design of the America's Center expansion breaks down the 414,000-square-foot facility into appropriately scaled urban elements, including a crescent, a rotunda, and a corner turret. These elements mark the building's path as it weaves through the urban fabric.

The Edward Jones Dome joins America's Center to form one of the country's most versatile sports and convention facilities. The playing field can quickly be converted into an 185,000-square-foot exhibition space.

Brick, the major material, is accented with ornamental terracotta panels and cast stone treatments reminiscent of surrounding city architecture, most notably the Wainwright Building designed by architect Louis Sullivan.

1

2

1 The exhibit hall connects to a circulation spine, which culminates in the dramatic entry rotunda boasting terrazzo floors and a hand-rendered plaster dome
2 The brick, terracotta and cast stone exterior relates to the notable architecture surrounding the center
3 The crescent-shaped design offers a welcoming architectural embrace intended to draw people to the center
4 The center includes an auditorium lecture hall with multiple levels of seating
5 The architectural design and materials of the center reflect its historic surroundings
6 The center boasts an open feel, with natural lighting and convenient access to meeting rooms and conference facilities

6

78 America's Center Expansion and Edward Jones Dome Hellmuth, Obata + Kassabaum

Iowa Events Center

Design/Completion 2001/2004
Des Moines, Iowa, U.S.A.
City of Des Moines
1 million square feet
Concrete super structure, steel roof
Open-joint stone wall system, brick, open-joint aluminum plate wall system,
glass curtain wall, lead-coated copper roof

1

The Iowa Events Center is a major component of downtown Des Moines' revitalization. The design incorporates the half-century-old Veterans Memorial Auditorium with two state-of-the-art facilities: Wells Fargo Arena and Hy-Vee Exhibition Hall.

Located along the Des Moines River, the Iowa Events Center will provide excellent views of the downtown skyline and the Iowa State Capitol. The stone-and-brick exterior complements the existing auditorium while featuring large expanses of glass.

The new arena's multi-purpose design will enable it to host all forms of indoor sports, concerts, and entertainment. The new hall will provide 250,000 square feet of flexible exhibition space.

1 The new exhibition hall is directly linked with Vets Auditorium, which will provide additional exhibit space along with more than 7,000 seats
2 The arena will offer a number of premium seating options for a variety of event types
3 The stone-and-brick exterior complements the existing auditorium while featuring large expanses of glass

2

3

Anaheim Convention Center Expansion

Design/Completion 1995/2001
Anaheim, California, U.S.A.
City of Anaheim
850,000 square feet
Steel frame
Metal and glass curtain wall, aluminum lath

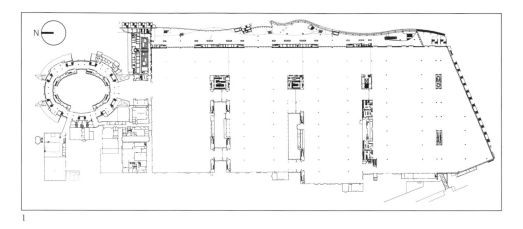

1

The need for more space and a fresh image for its convention center motivated the City of Anaheim to develop a new master plan for the facility.

Phase I included an 85,000-square-foot expansion to an exhibit hall. Phase II consisted of a new 200,000-square-foot exhibit hall, 145,000 square feet of meeting rooms and a ballroom, and 200,000 square feet of prefunction space.

The design reflects a Southern California "Spirit of Place." Forms, colors, and materials are rooted in the land, architecture, and culture found in and around Anaheim, which offers mountains, deserts, beaches, highways, farming, and Native American culture.

2

1 Detailed drawing of the main floor plan
2 The new entry features a vehicular arrival plaza marking the symbolic heart of the center
3 A new "front door" updates the image of the facility while encouraging residents of the community to recognize the convention center as an important civic structure
4 A continuous reception spine directs traffic to expanded exhibit halls and new meeting rooms on three levels
5 The facility's design ensures that large groups of people can move efficiently and comfortably throughout the facility
6 Color, materials, lighting, plantings, and graphics all enhance the concept of Southern California as a paradise of mountains, ocean, and desert

3

5

6

Indiana Convention Center Renovation and Expansion

Design/Completion 1991/1994 (Phase I), 1998/2001 (Phase II)
Indianapolis, Indiana, U.S.A.
Indiana Capital Development Board
200,000 square feet Phase I; 400,000 square feet Phase II
Steel frame
Indiana limestone, Minnesota Kasota stone, brick, curtain wall

1   The design of the north facade relates to the nearby
    State Capitol, state office buildings, and a formal
    park
2   Classical details accent the facility's exterior
3   The glass-enclosed landings on the second level
    offer dramatic views of the city
4   The smaller scale brick facade with limestone
    accents complements a red-brick district highlighted
    by Union Station on the east

The Indiana Convention Center expansion focused on providing flexible convention space and updating the Center's image.

The initial expansion occurred on two sides of the existing Center, facing two distinctly different parts of the city. Indiana limestone with brick detailing and classical formality reflect the north side's context, while smaller-scaled brick and limestone accents echo the east side. Rotated glass cube atriums at both ends of the Center allow dramatic views toward the Capitol.

A second expansion rotated the exhibit halls 90 degrees to provide access along a long prefunction gallery and park while adding 200,000 square feet of exhibit space.

1

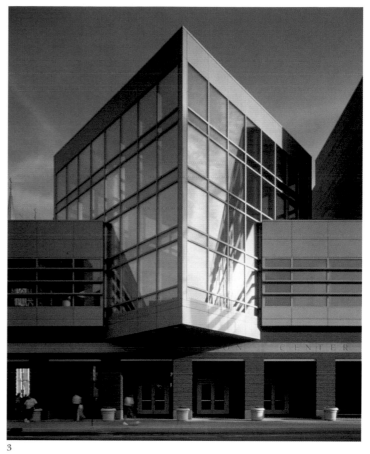

2

3

4

Fort Worth Convention Center Expansion

Design/Completion 1999/2002 (Phase I), 2003 (Phase II)
Fort Worth, Texas, U.S.A.
City of Fort Worth
275,000 square feet
Steel and concrete frame
Brick and curtain wall
Associate architect: Carter & Burgess

The design for the 275,000-square-foot Forth Worth Convention Center expansion reduces the apparent scale by developing an exterior streetscape of smaller facades reminiscent of the scale of the city's downtown.

To reflect a sophisticated blend of old and new Fort Worth, the design team created a highly articulated brick-and-glass facade reflecting a "Fort Worth vernacular" along the length of the center.

A circular "star tower" crowns the entrance on the southwest corner. This primarily glass tower is topped with a large 10-point star. The tower offers an open view to the ground level for those standing on the inside mezzanine.

1

2

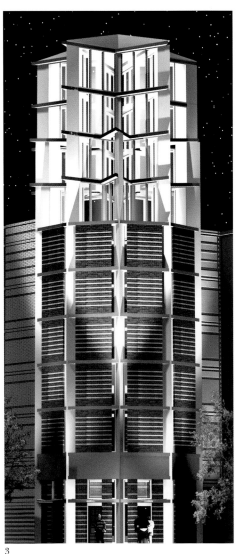

1   The design solution for this large project included the development of a unique exterior "streetscape"
2   The convention center features a pattern of smaller facades to reduce the apparent scale of the facility
3   The circular glass "star tower" crowns the center's entrance

3

Public and Institutional

Utah Consolidated Courts Complex, Salt Lake City, Utah, U.S.A.

United States Embassy, Moscow

Design/Completion 1994/2000
Moscow, Russia
United States Department of State (Office of Building Operations)
220,000 square feet
Re-use of a portion of existing precast concrete structure combined with
new steel frame with precast concrete
Limestone and glass curtain wall

1

The U.S. Department of State selected HOK, in association with Weidlinger Associates, to lead a consortium of firms responsible for this multidisciplinary design effort.

The building incorporates innovative security devices and extensive shielding systems.

The unique sensitivity of this project required all contractor office facilities to receive Top Secret clearance and all team members involved with classified information to gain Top Secret personnel clearance.

Security reasons prevent the release of additional information.

1 Front elevation
2 Glass curtain wall
3 Limestone and glass curtain wall
4 Stair in main lobby

2

3

Hellmuth, Obata + Kassabaum **United States Embassy, Moscow 87**

Federal Reserve Bank of Minneapolis Headquarters and Operations Center

Design/Completion 1991/1997
Minneapolis, Minnesota, U.S.A.
Federal Reserve Bank of Minneapolis
618,000 square feet
Poured reinforced concrete structure
Buff-colored brick, smooth and rough-cut Minnesota Mankato-Kasota stone, stainless steel, green-tinted glass

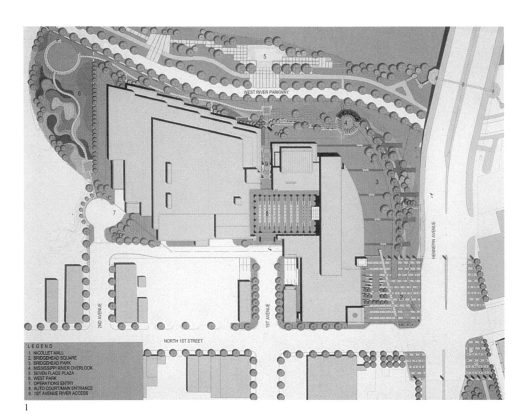

1

2

Operational simplicity, security of the highest order, and reverence for the historic site were the goals guiding the design of the new headquarters and operations center for the Federal Reserve Bank of Minneapolis. The complex overlooks the Mississippi River on the site of Minneapolis's original settlement and first public square.

The design respects the bank's tradition of stability, security, and strength. The building combines brick (the primary material in the adjacent North Warehouse District) and Kasota stone (indigenous to Minnesota) with crisp contemporary detailing in precast concrete. A curved glass wall faces a landscaped plaza, the river, and the Hennepin Avenue Bridge.

The dual mission of the Federal Reserve is expressed by dividing the facility into a seven-story office building with a 222-foot clock tower and a connected four-story operations center.

1   Site plan
2   View across Mississippi River showing full complex
3   View of office tower and plaza
Following pages:
    East elevation showing park connection to river

3

5 Employee dining area overlooking Mississippi River
6 Lobby
7 Plaza
8 Executive office

5

6

7

National Wildlife Federation Headquarters

Design/Completion 1998/2000
Reston, Virginia, U.S.A.
National Wildlife Federation
95,000 square feet
Steel structure
Split face concrete block, low-E glass, profiled metal panel, wood, stone,
natural and renewable interior products
Project consultant: William McDonough + Partners

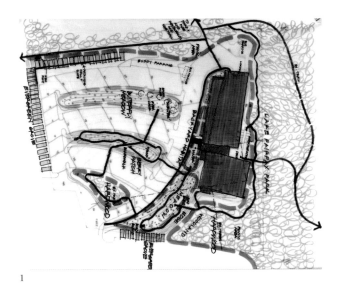

1

The new National Wildlife Federation (NWF) headquarters building is adjacent to Lake Fairfax Park in Reston, Virginia.

The goal was to follow a "common sense and common ground" approach to conservation: to create an inspiring, healthy workplace with modern communication tools.

NWF wanted its new headquarters to demonstrate sensible stewardship of financial resources. The design team used a rigorous payback analysis to select "state of-the-shelf" sustainable technologies and materials.

The American Institute of Architects (AIA) Committee on the Environment named the NWF headquarters building as one of the "Top 10 Green Projects" in 2002.

3

1   Segment plan
2   Multiple materials create an interesting facade
3   Library

2

Sam M. Gibbons U.S. Courthouse

Design/Completion 1992/1998
Tampa, Florida, U.S.A.
U.S. General Services Administration
438,000 square feet
Cast-in-place concrete structure with post-tensioned beams
Architectural precast concrete, cast-in-place concrete, aluminum curtain wall and metal panel system, Georgia gray granite

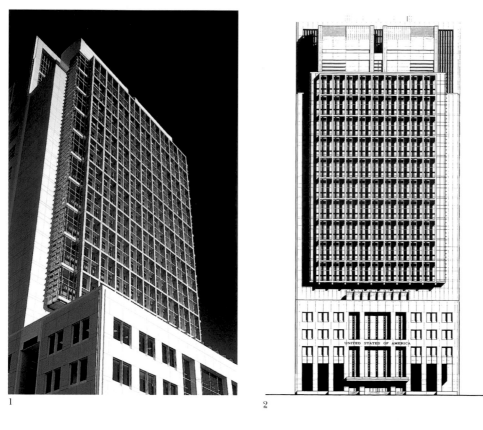

1

2

Providing an efficient layout and an environmentally sensitive building while complementing an adjacent courthouse were the primary goals directing the design of this new U.S. courthouse.

The design is formal and carefully proportioned, reflecting the function of the spaces inside. Set back from Florida Avenue, the new courthouse creates a pedestrian plaza that mirrors that of the existing courthouse.

The new building contains 17 courtrooms, judges' suites, and clerk operation areas. Upper floors house two courts on each floor, as well as judges' chambers. The special proceedings courtroom is on the top floor. The lower six floors provide office and support space.

Natural lighting, passive solar control, and environmentally sensitive building materials are all integral to the energy-conserving design. Building materials were carefully selected to be nontoxic and renewable, and have low embodied energy. The building's high-efficiency MEP systems and other sustainable features have earned the courthouse an award from the U.S. Department of Energy.

1   Detail of tower
2   Entry elevation
3   Typical District Court chamber
4   View through skylight of atrium

3

Thomas F. Eagleton U.S. Courthouse

Design/Completion 1992/1998
St. Louis, Missouri, U.S.A.
U.S. General Services Administration
1 million square feet
Poured concrete core structure with steel framing
Limestone, precast concrete, glass, stainless steel

A combined expression of regionalism and federalism was key to the design of the new Thomas F. Eagleton U.S. Courthouse. Columns and domes—trademarks of St. Louis architecture found in monumental buildings throughout the city—are features of the new courthouse.

Limestone and precast concrete cladding are punctuated with large expanses of glass, blending traditional and contemporary design themes. The stainless steel dome reflects both the moody skies of the Midwest and the material of the Gateway Arch.

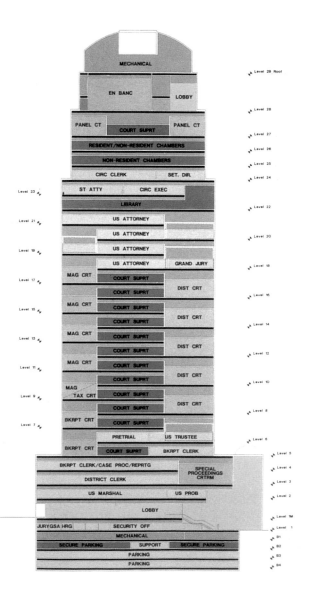

1   2

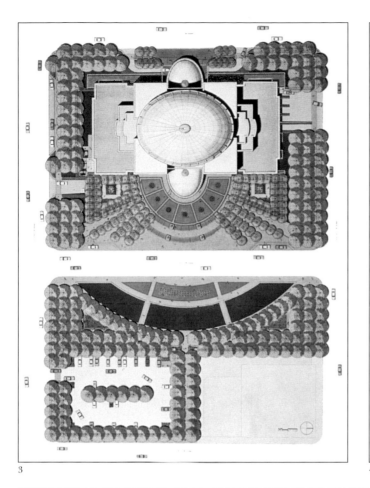

3

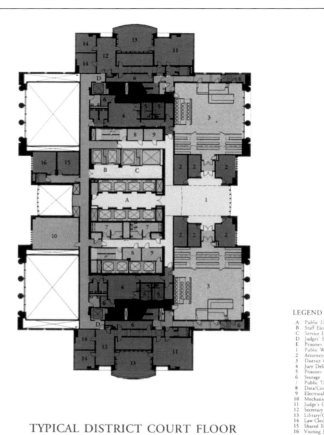

TYPICAL DISTRICT COURT FLOOR
LEVELS 8, 10, 12, 14, 16

LEGEND

A   Public Elevators
B   Staff Elevators
C   Service Elevators
D   Judges Elevator
E   Prisoner Elevator
1   Public Waiting
2   Attorney/Client Conf.
3   District Courtroom
4   Jury Deliberation
5   Prisoner Holding
6   Storage
7   Public Toilets
8   Data/Comm. Closet
9   Electrical Closet
10 Mechanical Equipment
11 Judge's Chamber
12 Secretary
13 Library/Conference
14 Law Clerk
15 Shared Resource Center
16 Visiting Judge's Chamber

4

1   View from northeast
2   Stacking diagram
3   Site plan
4   Typical District Court floor
5   Rotunda topped by stainless steel dome

5

6 Courtroom with view of St. Louis Arch
7 Windows flank Circuit Court lobby
8 Main lobby
9 Elevator lobby

6

7

8

9

Federal Reserve Bank of Cleveland Headquarters and Operations Center

Design/Completion 1993/1998
Cleveland, Ohio, U.S.A.
Federal Reserve Bank of Cleveland
430,000 square feet
Concrete structure below grade, steel frame above grade
Etowah Fleuri marble from Georgia on precast back-up, glass, painted metal, terracotta medallions
Associate architect: van Dijk, Pace, Westlake & Partners

The design goal for the renovation of this historically significant building and its connecting addition was to express stability, tradition, integrity, and the Federal Reserve's "corporate" identity—but with an eye to the future.

A compatible relationship between the existing building and a new 270,000-square-foot annex was established through the use of complementary materials, scale, setbacks, and forms.

The addition re-interprets the existing building's disposition of elements to reflect its new uses and expression as a modern building. A glass atrium links the two buildings with minimal disturbance of the bank's original facade.

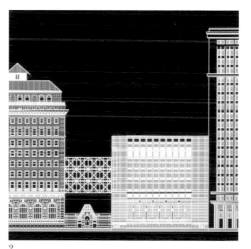

1 New 270,000-square-foot annex
2 Axonometric
3 Glass atrium linking historic building with addition
4 Facade detail

Alfred A. Arraj U.S. Courthouse Annex

Design/Completion 1995/2002
Denver, Colorado, U.S.A.
U.S. General Services Administration
343,000 square feet
Steel frame
Limestone, glass, aluminum
Architect of record: Anderson Mason Dale P.C.
Design architect: Hellmuth, Obata + Kassabaum

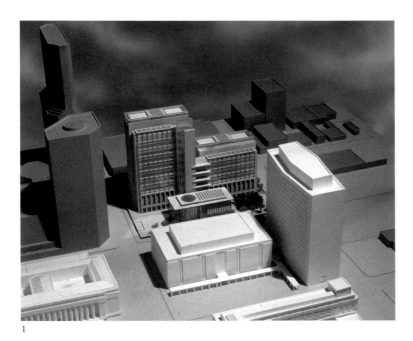

1

The U.S. Courthouse expansion in Denver projects an image of dignity and respect while reflecting the city's architectural heritage.

This courthouse tower and low pavilion are proportionally balanced in response to the surrounding Federal District and urban context. The tower, a series of vertically oriented rectangular planes, celebrates its top with an open framework and a floating horizontal roof of photovoltaic panels.

An arrangement of geometric forms under a larger horizontal roof, the two-story pavilion acts as the frontispiece to the entire complex while recalling the traditional town square courthouse.

EAST ELEVATION

0 10' 20'   40'   80'

2

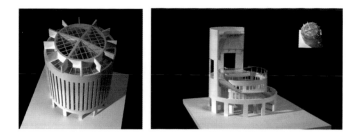

1 Aerial view
2 East elevation
3 Building section, Special Proceedings Pavilion
4 Site plan
5 Typical District Court floor

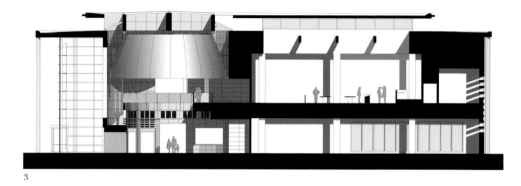

3

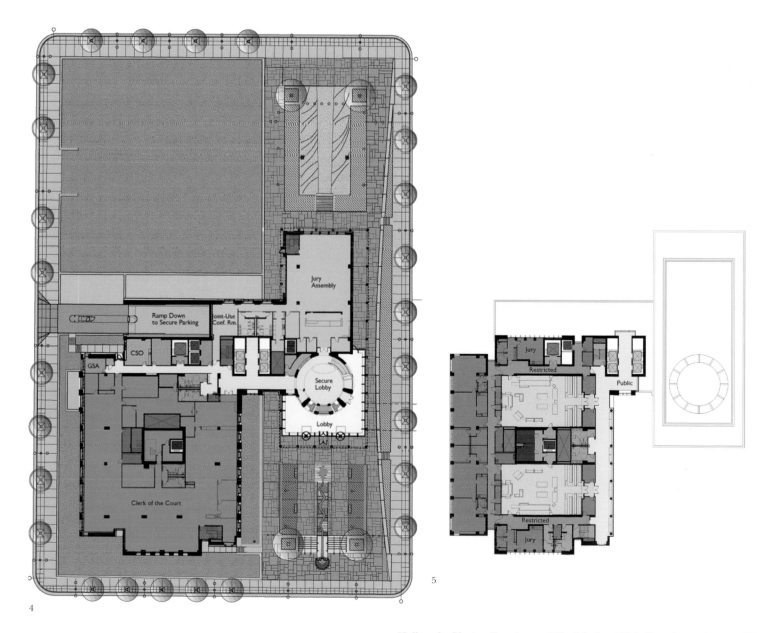

4

5

St. Louis County Justice Center

Design/Completion 1995/1998
Clayton, Missouri, U.S.A.
St. Louis County
503,000 square feet
Concrete frame
Brick, limestone, glass
Associate architect: Sverdrup

1

2

Driven by the need to consolidate its criminal justice facilities, St. Louis County hired Sverdrup and HOK to design a new 1,232-bed justice center across the street from its existing courthouse.

The site, adjacent to major commercial structures in downtown Clayton, demanded a creative approach. The challenge of making a good neighbor of what is essentially a detention facility in an upscale neighborhood resulted in a design that features large glass areas and has the appearance of an office building.

The upper five floors containing inmate housing are faced in brick and glass curtain wall. The brick is similar in color to that used in the County's existing courthouse and administration buildings, visually expanding the government center campus. The glass curtain wall responds to the context of neighboring high-rises.

The lower three floors housing office and support functions are clad in limestone. A second-level walkway connecting the new building to the courthouse is divided into side-by-side corridors, one for the screened public and the other for the secure transfer of in-custody defendants.

1   Main entry facade showing connection to existing
    courthouse
2   Detail of glass curtain wall
3   Plan of typical direct-supervision floor
4   Courtroom
5   Dayroom surrounded by inmate cells

1 Unit control
2 Sallyport
3 Unit administration
4 Multipurpose room
5 Visiting
6 Service chase
7 Dayroom
8 Recreation
9 Accessible cell
10 Standard cell

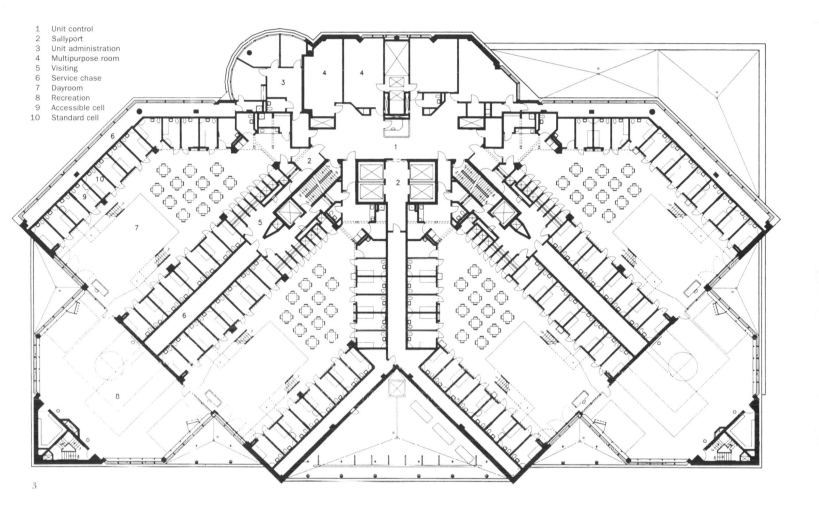

3

4

5

Phoenix Municipal Courthouse

Design/Completion 1996/1999
Phoenix, Arizona, U.S.A.
City of Phoenix
330,000 square feet
Steel frame
Red Arizona sandstone, precast concrete
Associate architect: DMJM

1　Main entry
2　Main lobby
3　Site plan
4　Close-up of facade showing shading devices

1

A high-quality courthouse with superior customer access and ease of use was the design objective for the new municipal courthouse in Phoenix.

The design blends the dignity and permanence appropriate to the judicial mission with a warmth rarely found in civic architecture.

The building responds to the intense heat of the Southwestern climate by turning its shoulder to the southern and western sun and by using shading devices along with native materials and landscaping. The building's turned axis also allowed for the preservation of the historic Walker Building, which has become an important site amenity.

3

2

4

Aviation

Orlando International Airport Airside 2, Orlando, Florida, U.S.A.

King Khaled International Airport

Design/Completion 1975/1983
Riyadh, Saudi Arabia
Ministry of Defense & Aviation, Presidency of Civil Aviation, IAP
3,300,000 square feet
Steel frame structure
Metal, concrete
Joint venture with Bechtel

1

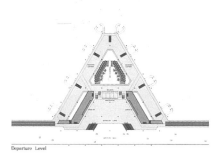

Departure Level

2

3

4

A thorough study of Islamic architecture informed the design solution for King Khaled International Airport. The extensive use of geometry in Islamic architectural tradition inspired a design that relies on the triangle shape as the overall foundation on which forms are built.

The four triangular-shaped passenger terminals (two domestic and two international) feature atria with fountains and green plants. A mosque for 5,000 worshippers inside and another 5,000 outside serves as the focal point of the entire terminal complex.

A royal pavilion functions as a VIP terminal and as a palace for the King. Set apart, beneath a triangular roof similar to that of the other terminals, the pavilion centers on a large reception hall. Around the main hall are a large suite for the King, two smaller suites for visiting dignitaries and other royal family members, and a large theater for press conferences. Below this level is a small air terminal with arrival and departure facilities for the entourages of visiting dignitaries.

Landscaped roadways, malls, covered arcades, plazas, gardens, fountains, and waterways link the various buildings.

5

1 Site plan
2 Floor plan of departure level
3 Aerial view
4 Exterior view of gate
5 View across typical waiting area
6 View under dome in mosque

6

East Terminal at Lambert-St. Louis International Airport

Design/Completion 1996/1999
St. Louis, Missouri, U.S.A.
St. Louis Airport Authority
225,200 square feet
Steel truss and frame structure with composite concrete slabs
Metal, glass

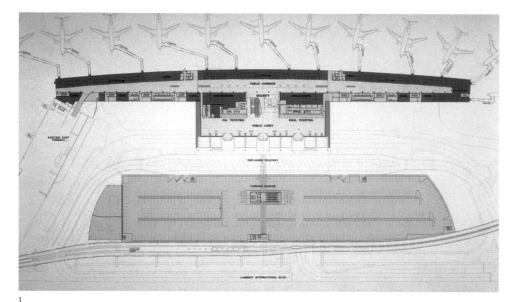

1

After designing the original 1957 Lambert-St. Louis International Airport Terminal, HOK has designed a 12-gate East Terminal that includes ticketing, baggage claim, concourse, roadways, and a parking structure.

The passenger-friendly plan emphasizes clarity of direction, with an open entry area providing visual access through the facility. This glass-enclosed entry creates an airy, relaxed atmosphere and is topped by a distinctive roof shape that symbolizes the exciting dynamic of flight.

2

3

4

5

Fukuoka International Airport International Passenger Terminal

Design/Completion 1992/1999
Fukuoka, Japan
Fukuoka Airport Building Co.
710,000 square feet
Steel frame
Glass/aluminum curtain wall, metal roof
Associate architects: Azusa Sekkei, Mishima Architects, and MHS Planners

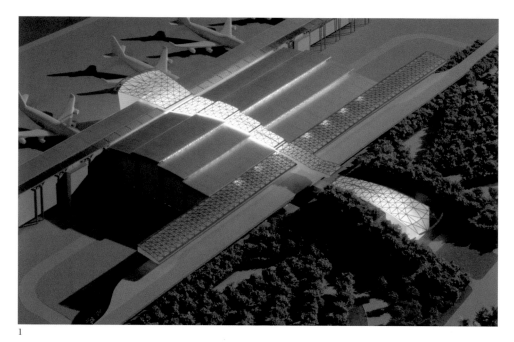

HOK and Azusa Sekkei, along with Mishima Architects and MHS Planners, designed a US $280-million international passenger terminal at Japan's rapidly expanding Fukuoka International Airport. The terminal was designed as a new "gateway to Asia."

The terminal integrates lightweight, simple span structures and north-facing clerestories to provide spectacular views of nearby mountains. A gently curved roof composed of five airfoil-like shells is supported by exposed tube steel composite trusses. These trusses allow for deep overhangs on the east and west sides of the building and for a column-free spine in the center. This skylit spine acts as the main circulation hub.

1   Aerial view of model
2   Elevation showing curved roof with airfoil-like shells
3   Close-up showing deep overhangs
4   Ticketing area
5   Sky-lit spine
6   Connection from ticketing area to lower-level concourse

3

4

5

6

Sendai International Airport
Domestic and International Passenger Terminal

Design/Completion 1994/1997
Sendai, Japan
Sendai Airport Terminal Co. Ltd.
475,000 square feet
Reinforced concrete structure with long-span steel truss roof system
Glass and metal exterior wall systems
Associate architect: Nikken Sekkei

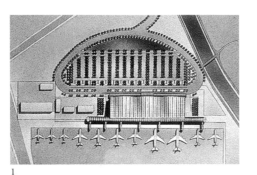

1

2

3

4

Conceived as a model for Japan's new regional airports, this two-level terminal accommodates domestic and international operations in a compact building with a single gateway identity.

Because the airport serves a recreational destination known for its lush green setting and unique island environment, the terminal was designed to reflect the serenity of the natural landscape. Domestic and international wings are connected by a central atrium under a gentle triple-wave roof. The roof's shape draws its inspiration from the surrounding mountain range, the lapping waves of the nearby coastline, and the aerodynamic forms of flight. From the mezzanine and the departure lounge, passengers view the airfield with the distant mountains as a scenic backdrop.

By the year 2000, the terminal is expected to serve an estimated 3.3 million passengers annually.

1 Site plan
2 Pedestrian skywalk linking parking to central atrium
3 View of main entry and drop-off area
4 Night view of drop-off area
5 Mezzanine level
6 Ticketing area
Following page:
 Gated seating within tubular concourse

5

6

Hellmuth, Obata + Kassabaum **Sendai International Airport Domestic and International Passenger Terminal** 113

Oakland International Airport Terminal Expansion

Design/Completion 2000/2008
Oakland, California, U.S.A.
Port of Oakland
1 million square feet
Steel frame
Composite aluminum panels, energy efficient tinted-glass curtain wall
Joint venture with Kwan Henmi Architecture/Planning, Inc.,
Powell & Partners Architects, and KPA Consulting Engineers, Inc.

1

The vision for Oakland's US $900-million expansion program is to make the airport more passenger-focused and traveler-friendly while increasing the passenger capacity by 50 percent. The number of annual passengers will soon grow from 10 million to 14 million, with air cargo increasing from 700,000 to 1 million metric tons.

The program encompasses multiple major projects, including the reconfiguration of two existing single-level terminals into one two-level facility with a double-decked arrivals/departures roadway system, a 6,000-car, six-level parking structure, and two new concourses with 12 additional gates.

1   Site plan
2   Computer-generated drawing of bridge view
3   Aerial view of model

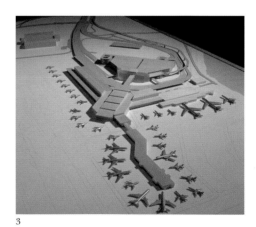

2

3

Education

Whitehead Biomedical Research Building at Emory University, Atlanta, Georgia, U.S.A.

King Saud University

Design/Completion 1975/1984
Riyadh, Saudi Arabia
Ministry of Education, President of the Supreme Council of the University
6.5 million square feet (2,400 acres)
Concrete structure
Precast concrete
HOK+4 Consortium: Hellmuth, Obata + Kassabaum; Gollins Melvin Ward
Partnership; Caudill Rowlett Scott; Syska & Hennessy; Dames & Moore

1

As one of the world's largest building projects at the time, King Saud University was planned for an initial population of 21,000 students, with the capacity to expand to accommodate twice that number. The HOK+4 Consortium carried out the design, engineering, and construction administration of the university campus of ten colleges.

The contemporary design reflects the traditional Najd architecture of Central Arabia. Academic buildings are interconnected by covered circulation spines and enclosed pedestrian malls. At the core is a forum surrounded by the library, auditorium, university center, and administration building.

The standardized precast concrete building system provides flexibility for easy expansion.

1   Entrance to overall campus
2   Site plan
3   Enclosed pedestrian malls connect the buildings
4   College building viewed from covered walkway
5   Interior plaza
6   Part of second floor plan

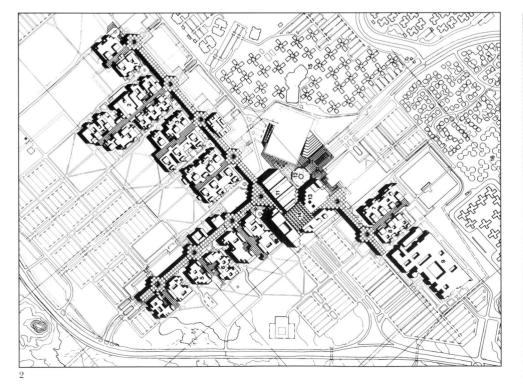

2

3

4

5

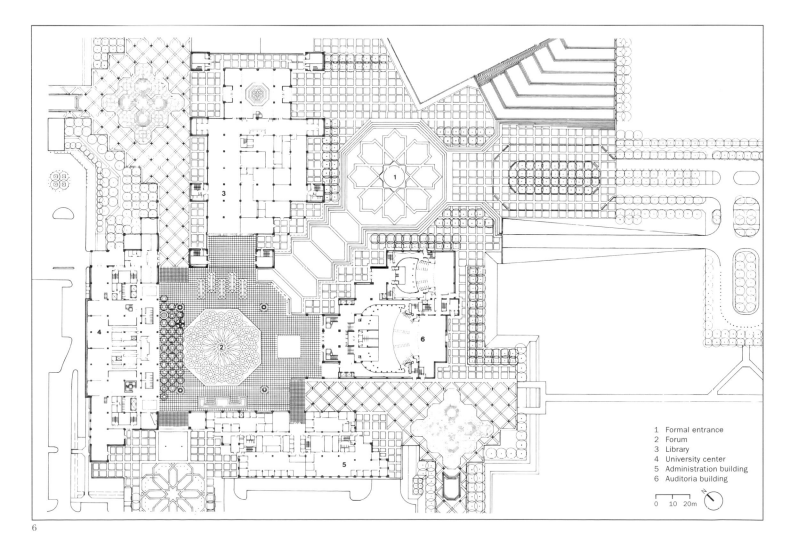

1 Formal entrance
2 Forum
3 Library
4 University center
5 Administration building
6 Auditoria building

0 10 20m

6

Genetics and Plant Biology Center

Design/Completion 1984/1990
Berkeley, California, U.S.A.
University of California
187,500 square feet
Cast-in-place concrete structure
Granite, poured concrete, clay tile, copper

1

2

The University of California at Berkeley's Genetics and Plant Biology Center includes two adjacent buildings, one for research and one for teaching. The facility was designed to consolidate the university's plant sciences functions allowing faculty to share equipment and collaborate on research. The university also wanted a high-quality environment that would help to recruit and retain top researchers.

The research building contains 38 generic research laboratories, compactly arranged on a quadruple-loaded corridor around a central circulation core. This layout creates shared support spaces and minimizes the distance between labs, encouraging interaction among researchers.

The teaching building includes teaching laboratories and general classrooms, a large lecture hall, and a food service facility.

The main entrances of the five-story research building and two-story classroom facility face each other and are linked by a walkway that preserves an existing pedestrian route and views of San Francisco Bay. An open central stairway with a large skylight provides natural light to all levels. Large windows at the ends of corridors provide a sense of openness.

1   Looking east (research building on left)
2   Typical research lab
3   Lecture hall in teaching building
4   South elevation of teaching building

3

4

Schapiro Center for Engineering and Physical Science Research

Design/Completion 1988/1992
New York, New York, U.S.A.
Columbia University, New York State
200,000 square feet
Poured-in-place concrete structure
Precast concrete and metal

1

Columbia University's desire for a high-technology research center guided the design of the Schapiro Center for Engineering and Physical Science Research. The building provides the university with flexible space for state-of-the-art research in computer sciences, telecommunications, microelectronics, robotics, and bioengineering.

The building's materials, patterns, and details reflect both its high-tech function and the historic McKim, Mead & White-designed Columbia campus. As the northern terminus of the central campus axis, the building is deliberately monumental and classically Beaux Arts in proportion and roof profile. Punched openings and stone-like detailing recall neighboring campus and community buildings.

The Schapiro Center opens the campus to the community through original gates, brought out of storage and refurbished to fit into the high-tech materials of metal, ceramic patterned glass, and high-capacity tube truss bridges.

1   West side of building
2   Terrace level plan
3   Exterior facing campus plaza
4   Site plan
5   Exterior facing street
6   Auditorium

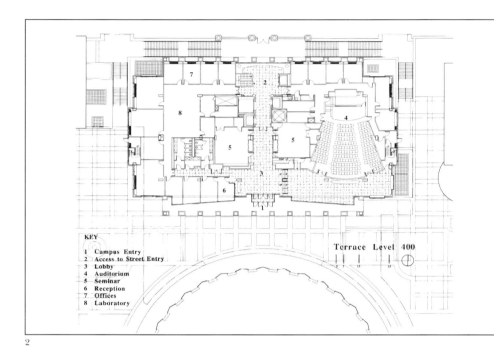

2

3

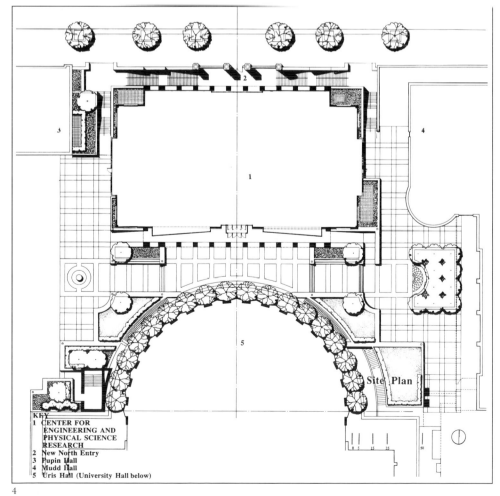

KEY
1 Campus Entry
2 Access to Street Entry
3 Lobby
4 Auditorium
5 Seminar
6 Reception
7 Offices
8 Laboratory

Terrace Level 400

KEY
1 CENTER FOR
  ENGINEERING AND
  PHYSICAL SCIENCE
  RESEARCH
2 New North Entry
3 Pupin Hall
4 Mudd Hall
5 Uris Hall (University Hall below)

Site Plan

4

5

6

George Bush Presidential Library Center

Design/Completion 1991/1997
College Station, Texas, U.S.A.
Texas A&M University
300,000 square feet
Poured-in-place concrete and steel structure
Texas pink granite, limestone

1

In 1991, President George Bush stated his wish that the George Bush Presidential Library Center be "a place for visitors to feel comfortable, not a monument. Something that would blend into the A&M campus."

With the ex-President's vision in mind, the complex is designed as a campus within a campus, with the center's three buildings—library archives, conference center, and academic facility—placed to take advantage of the natural beauty of the 90-acre site. A multilevel pedestrian plaza, complete with amenities including fountains and sculptures, provides dramatic links between buildings.

The cornerstone of the complex, the 79,400-square-foot Presidential Library, embodies both traditional federal design influences and the native Southwest architectural vernacular. The two styles are combined in a spirit of Modernism, chosen to express the former President's focus on international matters during his 30 years of public service. Native Texas granite and limestone are incorporated into all three buildings.

The library's glass entry reveals a 50-foot-high lobby crowned by a skylit rotunda, the connecting point for the one-story exhibition wing and the three-story archival wing. Beyond the lobby are a 150-seat orientation theater and views of researchers at work on the archive's glass-encased second level.

2

1	Site plan	4	Exhibition wing
2	Multilevel plaza	5	Orientation theater
3	Rotunda skylight	6	Library showing archives and plaza

3

4

5

6

Collin County Community College

Design/Completion 1986/1989
Plano, Texas, U.S.A.
Collin County, Texas
385,000 square feet
Steel structure
Brick, tile
Associate architect: Corgan Associates

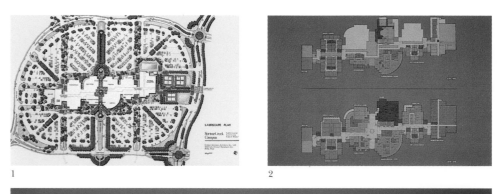

1

2

3

The primary goal for Collin County Community College, north of Dallas, was to design a climate-controlled campus that would generate a feeling of community among students.

HOK and Corgan Associates designed a gymnasium, a theater, a library, classrooms, offices, and a science laboratory under one roof, creating a mall-like atmosphere. Two enclosed, skylit interior streets branch north and south from a four-story atrium that forms the central courtyard. This central area provides space for community activities and connects the college's core facilities.

Rooms for noisier functions, including the music department and child-care center, are on streets that branch to the west of the central spine, while quieter rooms are on the east side. Each cluster of rooms functions as an acoustically buffered unit with its own secondary corridor.

Overhanging roof lines and specially designed skylights are tailored to the Texas climate, offering energy-efficient natural lighting without adding heat.

1   Landscape plan
2   Level one floor plan
3   Entry plaza
4   Exterior view
5   Theater

4

5

Houston Community College Health Science Center

Design/Completion 1997/1999
Houston, Texas, U.S.A.
Houston Community College
140,000 square feet
Steel structure
Precast concrete with limestone aggregate, metal panels, glass

This new Health Science Center in downtown Houston's Texas Medical Center supports an instructional curriculum for 26 health-related programs.

HOK's design for the five-story building is compatible, both in scale and materials, with neighboring structures, including the adjacent Shriners Hospital for Children.

A typical floor contains laboratory areas, classrooms arranged around an atrium, and staff administrative functions. Overlooking the atrium on each floor are student lounges.

The ground floor houses a library, auditorium, and computer center. These spaces are shared with community groups and linked to the Texas Medical Center and its related resources.

1 Main entry
2 Level five floor plan
3 Atrium showing student lounges on each floor

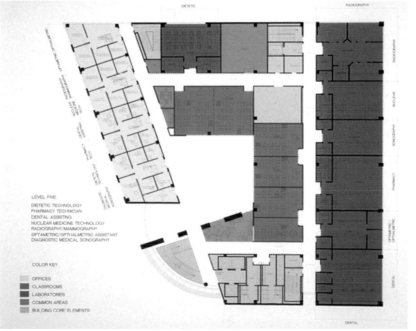

1

2   3

Texas Tech University Campus Master Plan

Design/Completion 1996/1997 (master plan)
Lubbock, Texas, U.S.A.
Texas Tech University
1,839 acres

The objective of the master plan for Texas Tech University was to respond to the challenges facing the university with guidelines for campus development. A freeway that bisected the campus was dividing the university's land uses and separating campus activities. The master plan integrates the freeway as an opportunity to develop a Texas Tech University theme and to establish a gateway for the institution.

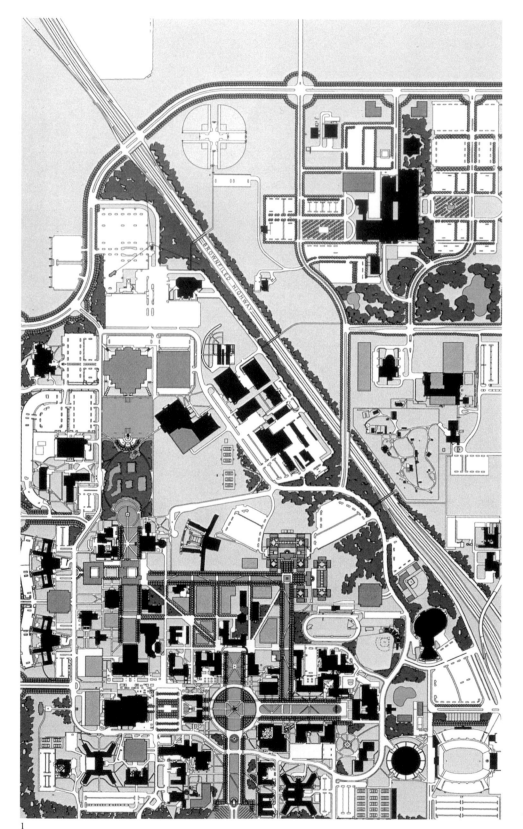

1

1   Texas Tech University Campus master plan

University of Wisconsin – Green Bay, Mary Ann Cofrin Hall

Design/Completion 1998/2001
Green Bay, Wisconsin, U.S.A.
University of Wisconsin
120,000 square feet
Steel structure
Brick, limestone, metal roof

This new classroom building accommodates half the university's classrooms, several of its environmental programs, and a distance education center.

The state wanted to make the project a model for energy conservation. The university went one step further and made the building a model for broader environmental issues, including energy conservation.

Using the U.S. Green Building Council's Leadership in Energy and Environmental Design rating system and *The HOK Guidebook to Sustainable Design* as tools, the team incorporated energy-conserving strategies such as full daylighting of all classrooms and common spaces, building-integrated photovoltaics, solar pre-heating, lighting systems integration, and many healthy materials.

1 Lobby off courtyard
2 East elevation
3 Level one floor plan
4 Aerial rendering

1

2

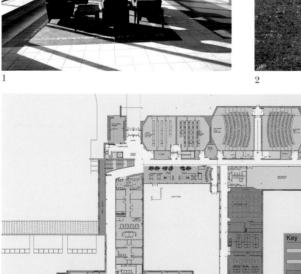

3

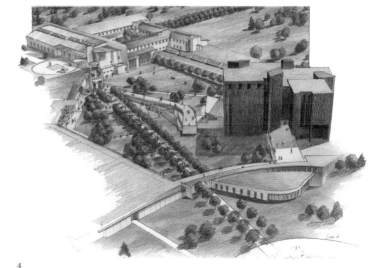

4

Georgia Institute of Technology
BEM Master Plan and Parker H. Petit Institute for Bioengineering and Bioscience

Design/Completion 1997/1999 (Parker H. Petit Institute)
Atlanta, Georgia, U.S.A.
Georgia Institute of Technology
150,000 square feet
Cast-in-place concrete structure
Brick, glass curtain wall

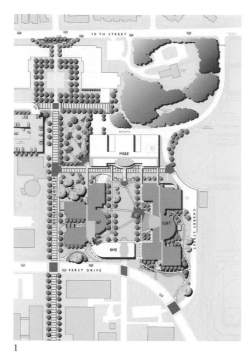

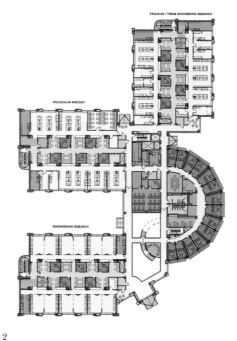

After master planning a new science complex for the Georgia Institute of Technology in 1996, HOK designed three of the four buildings that make up the 800,000-square-foot research campus. The state-of-the-art complex will become a national model for combining engineering and the sciences.

As the first step in the development of Georgia Tech's "biocomplex," the four-story Institute for Bioengineering and Bioscience facilitates the interdisciplinary research of faculty and their research groups, including students, bioengineers, and bioscientists.

Two other buildings currently are being designed and constructed around the quadrangle, which provides an open campus space. Ground-level arcades link the buildings.

1   BEM master plan
2   Typical floor plan, Petit Institute
3   West elevation, Petit Institute
4   Laboratory, Petit Institute

Science + Technology

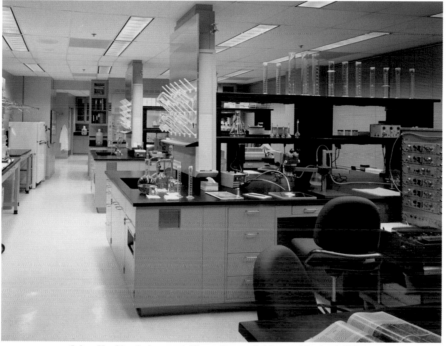

Johns Hopkins Asthma and Allergy Center, Baltimore, Maryland, U.S.A.

Bristol-Myers Squibb Headquarters and Research Campus

Design/Completion 1970/1999
Lawrenceville, New Jersey, U.S.A.
Bristol-Myers Squibb Company
More than 1,500,000 square feet
Steel structure
Limestone, brick

Since designing Bristol-Myers Squibb Company's headquarters and research campus in 1970, HOK's relationship with the pharmaceutical giant has been ongoing.

The original 700,000-square-foot facility was built on a 273-acre site in a largely residential area. Since then, HOK has designed several additions to that building as well as new laboratory buildings, a central utility building, and an animal facility. Scheduled for completion in 1999 is a four-story, 148,000-square-foot chemistry laboratory building, aptly named Module L for its L-shaped footprint.

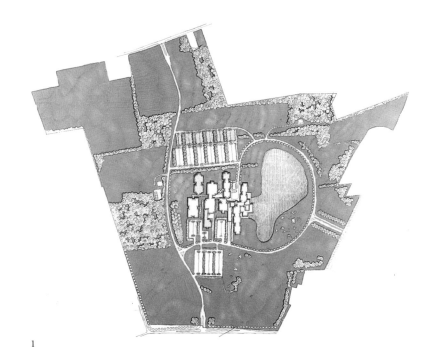

1

2

1 Site plan
2 Looking northeast at office building
3 Rendering of new chemistry laboratory building
4 View to lake from cafeteria
5 Looking north toward main building

3

4

5

Hellmuth, Obata + Kassabaum **Bristol-Myers Squibb Headquarters and Research Campus   131**

U.S. Environmental Protection Agency Campus

Design/Completion 1992/2001
Research Triangle Park, North Carolina, U.S.A.
U.S. Environmental Protection Agency
1,170,000 square feet
Steel and concrete pan joists structure
Precast concrete cladding

1

This new research and administration facility for the U.S. Environmental Protection Agency (EPA) supports a diverse group of scientists working together to protect the environment. The facility accommodates more than 2,000 people and contains 600 laboratory modules.

HOK's design embodies the EPA's goals for preserving the natural environment, conserving resources, preventing pollution, and fostering education about sustainable design.

The laboratories' built-in flexibility enables the EPA to keep pace with the constant changes in environmental science. Standard lab modules are paired with a flexible zone that accommodates lab or office use. Ventilation systems are designed to conserve energy while promoting the highest level of safety.

2

1 Campus site plan
2 West elevation
3 Model of site plan
4 Plaza leading to main entrance
5 Atrium

3

4

5

5

CDC Infectious Diseases Laboratory

Design/Completion 1996/2001
Atlanta, Georgia, U.S.A.
Center for Disease Control and Prevention
300,000 square feet (Phases I & II)
Cast-in-place concrete structure
Brick, metal panel/glass curtain wall, standing seam curved roof panels

Accommodating flexibility for a dynamic mix of 400 scientists was the intent for this new research building on the Center for Disease Control and Prevention's main campus in Atlanta.

The facility was designed in accordance with current CDC/NIH Guidelines for Biosafety in Microbiological and Biomedical Laboratories and within new federal guidelines for security of infectious agents.

Planned for flexibility, the new facility can handle the workload created by research programs with constantly changing requirements. Building systems, casework, and other systems are designed to accommodate changes quickly and easily.

2

3

1 Front facade
2 Cryogenetic freezers
3 Interstitial space

Hoffmann-La Roche Multidisciplinary Science Building

Design/Completion 1990/1994
Nutley, New Jersey, U.S.A.
Hoffmann-La Roche, Inc.
432,000 square feet
Structural steel
Precast concrete, glass

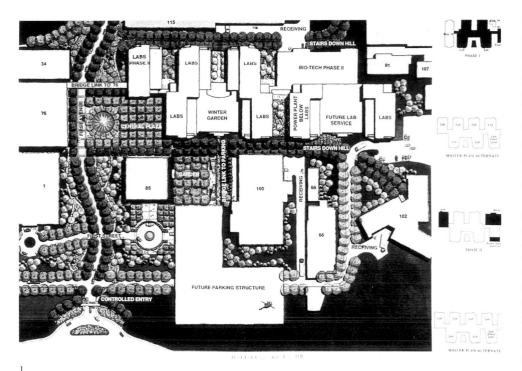

1

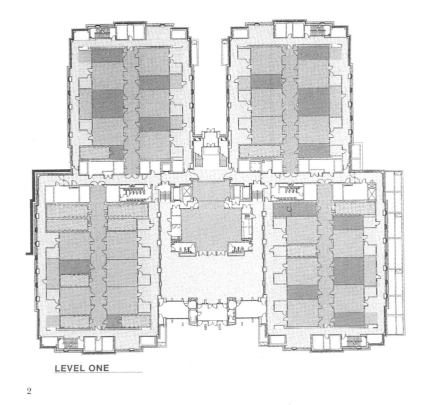

LEVEL ONE

2

The desire to provide a flexible, innovative research building that would help Hoffmann-La Roche maintain its position as one of the world's leading research-intensive pharmaceutical companies drove the design of the Multidisciplinary Science Building.

The six-story modular research building consists of four laboratory wings with 408 laboratories organized along a central spine. To promote interaction, laboratory wings are designed as research "neighborhoods," each with its own circulation, yet all linked to a main "street" and to central administration areas. A conference center along the central spine makes the science building the heart of the campus research community.

The integration of laboratories and process development areas—including molecular biology research, pharmaceutical research and development, and process laboratories—fosters a team approach from exploratory research through early product development, helping Roche speed new therapies to market. The large floor plan and modular, generic laboratory configurations permit flexibility to adapt to new technologies and accommodate the changing needs of research groups.

The building design helps unify the visual character of this complex site, which includes research, manufacturing, and administrative functions. The color, scale, massing, and details respect the campus fabric and provide a historic link to Roche's original facilities.

1   Site plan
2   Typical floor plan

3 Typical laboratory with connection to office space
4 Service corridor
5 Main entry facade
6 Typical laboratory
7 Atrium
Following page:
  Main entry

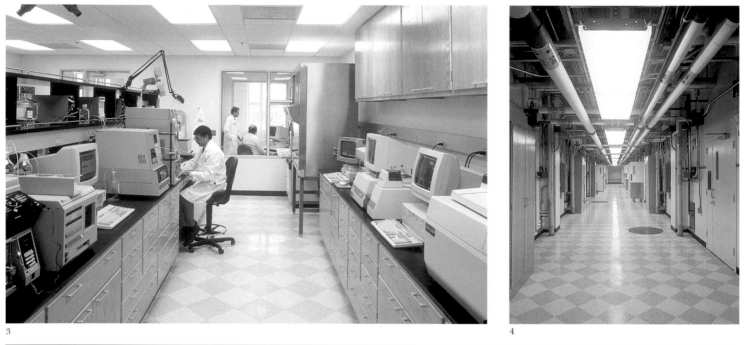

3

4

5

6

7

Corporate

VERITAS Software Headquarters Campus, Mountain View, California, U.S.A.

Levi's Plaza

Design/Completion 1977/1982
San Francisco, California, U.S.A.
Levi Strauss Corporation
816,000 square feet
Steel structure with reinforced concrete panels
Precast concrete panels faced in brick
Landscape architect: Lawrence Halprin and Associates

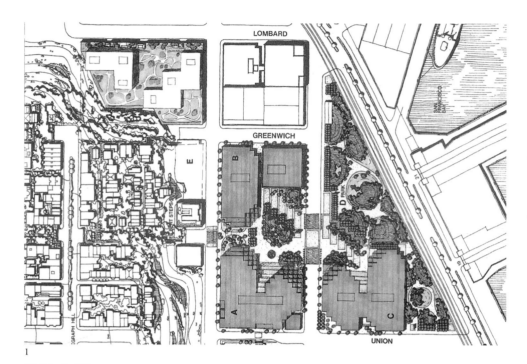

The design of this corporate headquarters for Levi Strauss Corporation was inspired by a desire to maintain a harmonious relationship with the historic area's residential and industrial buildings.

The three buildings are arranged around a large public park and face the San Francisco Bay. Massed and terraced to preserve views of the bay from scenic Telegraph Hill, Levi's Plaza complements the residential forms as they slope toward the waterfront. Balconies, bay windows, and the step-like brick facade harmonize with both neighboring Telegraph Hill homes and pre-1906 warehouse-turned-office buildings.

Time magazine praised HOK's design as one of the country's ten best in 1982.

1 Site plan
2 View of Telegraph Hill above corporate complex
3 Detail of building and park
4 Typical entry
5 Public park at center of complex

3

4

5

Apple Computer Headquarters Campus

Design/Completion 1990/1993
Cupertino, California, U.S.A.
Apple Computer, Inc.
846,000 square feet
Steel frame
Precast concrete, granite
Joint venture with Gensler, Studios Architecture, Holey Associates,
and Backen Arrigoni & Ross

1

2

Now a Cupertino landmark, Apple's campus houses the company's global R&D and office headquarters.

The six buildings are arranged around a central quadrangle that provides a series of outdoor gathering spaces.

Inside the buildings, Apple switched from its traditional open plan offices to a "caves and commons" approach in which researchers and programmers have private workspaces but share changeable, comfortable team areas.

The offices, laboratories, and conference areas were designed to promote interaction. By breaking down barriers between innovation and product development, Apple can speed its products to market.

3

4

1   Site plan
2   Courtyard
3   Main entry
4   View into central quadrangle
5   Atrium

AT&T Global Network Operations Center

Design/Completion 1996/2000
New Jersey, U.S.A.
AT&T
200,000 square feet
Steel frame
Steel, concrete, granite

1

The design for AT&T's network nerve center integrates technology while equipping the company with a "future-proof" facility.

At this "24-7" command center, AT&T coordinates the flow of data, voice, and wireless traffic across its global network. The center is built into a hillside, with two of the four levels underground.

An interior design theme based on the world's "seven rivers and seven continents" illustrates the multi-faceted cultures that make up the mosaic of civilization.

2

3

4

1 Entrance
2 Rotunda featuring floor mosaic with map of ancient world
3 Visitor observation room
4 High-tech console
5 Third level floor plan
6 Courtyard plan
7 View showing the three-story space with observation room on left
8 Visitor destination gallery

A - RECEPTION/LOBBY

B - ROTUNDA

C - PROMENADE

D - GALLERY

E - INTERNET CAFE

F - OBSERVATION RM.

G - AV/COMPUTER

H - OFFICES

OPEN TO FLOOR BELOW

0   60ft

5

6

7

8

Adobe Systems Headquarters

Design/Completion: 1994/1998 (Phase I & II), 2002/2003 (Phase III)
San Jose, California, U.S.A.
Adobe Systems
735,000 square feet (Phase I & II), 275,000 square feet (Phase III)
Steel structure
Granite, glass, stainless steel, aluminum

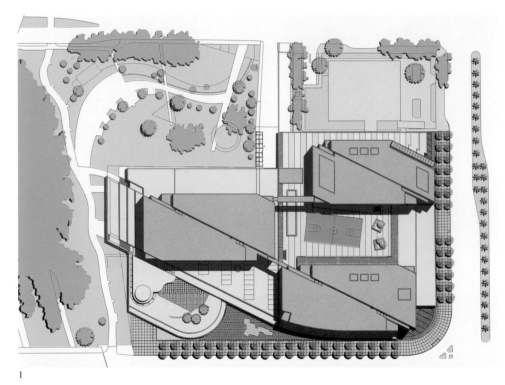

Adobe relocated 1,500 employees to a new high-rise in downtown San Jose. The design builds on the advantages of its urban location while injecting the best amenities of the less formal suburban settings to which employees were accustomed to working.

The two towers—18 stories and 16 stories, respectively—are bisected at a 45-degree angle by a quarter-mile-long hallway that forms a diagonal linking the two buildings. This "main street" acts as the organizing feature for common facilities. Pedestrian bridges link the structures on three floors.

HOK is now designing a Phase III 275,000-square-foot tower.

1   Site plan
2   View from nearby river park
3   Circulation corridor
4   Outdoor patio at tower base
5   Visitor lobby

1

2

3

4

5

Microsoft Augusta Campus

Design/Completion 1995/1998
Redmond, Washington, U.S.A.
Microsoft Corporation
560,000 square feet (office), 20,000 square feet (cafeteria), 610,000 square feet (parking)
Steel frame and poured-in-place concrete
Brick, precast concrete, metal, glass

1   Site plan
2   The campus maintains a low-scale character
3   Office buildings with commons building in right foreground
4   Open green space and central commons building reminiscent of a university campus

1

Satisfying the company's critical need for growth space was the intent of Microsoft's campus expansion.

Three office buildings surround open green space and a central commons building resembling that of a university campus.

Maintaining a low-scale character that complements the existing campus, the office buildings are four stories high, stepping down to three stories to accommodate the site's two zoning districts.

All buildings are connected. Each is divided into two parts linked by glazed bridges that enhance orientation within the large floor plates and provide light-filled informal meeting spaces.

2

3

4

Nortel Networks Brampton Centre

Design/Completion 1994/1996
Brampton, Ontario, Canada
Nortel Networks
1.2 million square feet
Steel frame
Brick, precast concrete, glass, aluminum

1

The conversion of a 1963 factory into a 1.2-million-square-foot, high-tech global headquarters provides a framework for communicating Nortel Networks' core values. A city planning approach breaks down the scale of the high-bay manufacturing space.

Boulevards, loops, sides streets, alleyways and shortcuts are marked by color-coded street signs and banners connecting the city's population. Different-sized neighborhoods made up of functional work groups are identified by strong visual elements. A series of piazzas and shops lining the main street help employees integrate work with their daily needs.

2

1 View of front facade
2 West-side expansion "Forum" meeting space
3 Typical "city" street
4 Green "utility trees" carry utilities to work areas through "branches"

3

4

Novell Western Region Offices

Design/Completion 1996/1999
San Jose, California, U.S.A.
Novell, Inc.
530,000 square feet
Steel structure
Granite, limestone

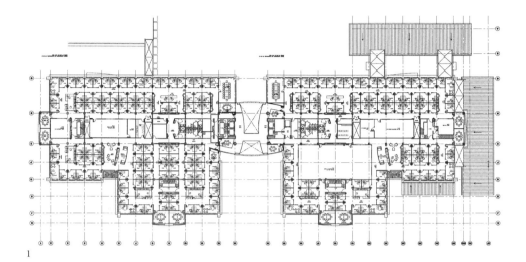

1

Novell consolidated employees into this campus in San Jose. The site is adjacent to the airport, Highway 101, and the light rail system. This prime location gives employees an easily accessible workplace in the heart of Silicon Valley.

The amenity-filled campus helps Novell satisfy the active lifestyle needs of its predominantly young workforce. Amenities include a glass-enclosed cafeteria, cafe, restaurant, espresso bar, sundries shop, dry cleaning services, ATM, fitness facilities, and outdoor recreational areas.

At 10-foot-by-12-foot, the private offices that make up 90 percent of the individual work areas are generous by Valley standards.

2

1 Floor plan
2 Buildings are sited to create a campus environment
3 The four-story atrium at the main entrance implies a strong presence
4 The combination of limestone and granite with a glass and metal panel curtain wall reflects stability with a fresh twist
5 Master site plan

Sun Microsystems Burlington Campus

Design/Completion 1996/1999
Burlington, Massachusetts, U.S.A.
Sun Microsystems
550,000 square feet
Composite steel structure with bracing
Brick and metal panels

1 Master site plan
2 This university-like campus is nestled into a rolling hillside
3 A solar clock tower announces Sun's presence in New England
4 The Sun store

1

This university-like campus is nestled into a rolling hillside on a 158-acre site outside Boston. A primary design goal was to improve employee collaboration and informal interaction.

The campus includes four low-rise buildings. All are interconnected by a one-level common facilities building housing the cafeteria, conference center, corporate library, and Sun store.

Large interconnecting stairs brightened by skylights and atrium entrances with clerestories are linked through a series of "main streets."

2

3

4

Capital One Renaissance Park Campus

Design/Completion 1994/2000
Tampa, Florida, U.S.A.
Capital One Financial Corporation
600,000 square feet
Poured-in-place concrete
Precast concrete, glass, aluminum sun shades

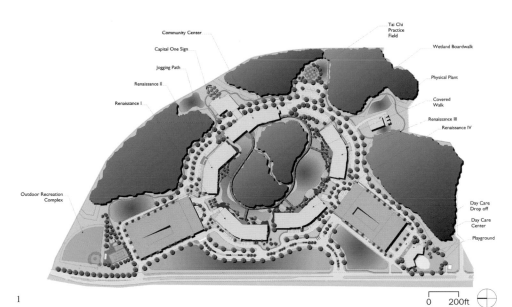

A primary goal for the Renaissance Park campus was to attract and keep employees by incorporating recreational and service amenities into the workday.

This new campus consists of three office buildings, a call center, and a community center amenities building.

Amenities include a health and fitness center, outdoor recreation complex and trails, learning center, media center, game room, Internet cafe and coffee bar, branch bank and ATM, and a food court and convenience store.

The campus was planned to preserve the wetlands and their associated upland buffers. The wetlands have become a focus of education and relaxation for employees.

1   Master site plan
2   Elevated walkways preserve the natural wetlands while allowing employees to interact with nature as they move between buildings
3   Covered walkways connect all buildings

Compaq Computer Campus Expansion

Design/Completion 1997/1998
Houston, Texas, U.S.A.
Compaq Computer Corporation
616,000 square feet
Steel and precast concrete structure
Silver aluminum panels, glass, precast panels and aluminum curtain wall (administration); composite steel panels, glass and precast panels (commons); composite steel panels and glass (visitors center)

1

2

These new buildings express Compaq's growth and global reach.

Two 10-story office buildings on the northern edge of the campus are connected at each level by a transparent walkway. An aluminum panel and glass curtain wall distinguish the buildings while complementing other campus structures.

A commons building invites interaction among staff, senior management, and customers in a casual environment.

Housed within the commons building are an 11,000-square-foot conference center, cafeteria, travel office, medical services, and other amenities. The facade opens westward, embracing covered walkways and a forest of pecan trees.

1   Visitors center exterior
2   Visitors center interior
3   Commons building entry
4   The commons center houses a variety of campus amenities
5   Campus site plan

3

4

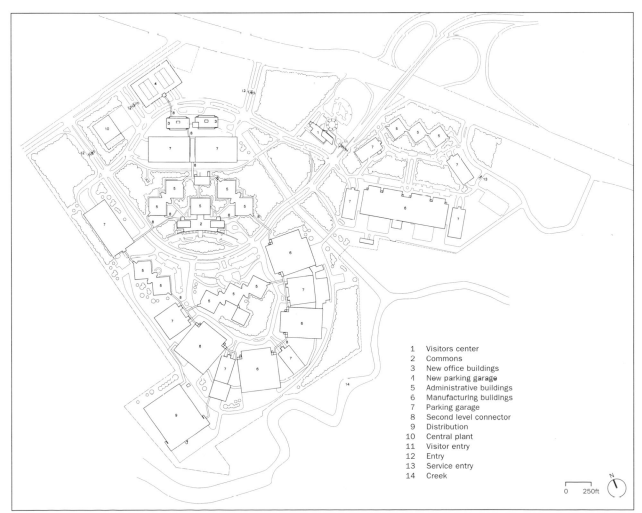

1   Visitors center
2   Commons
3   New office buildings
4   New parking garage
5   Administrative buildings
6   Manufacturing buildings
7   Parking garage
8   Second level connector
9   Distribution
10 Central plant
11 Visitor entry
12 Entry
13 Service entry
14 Creek

0   250ft

5

Tokyo Telecom Center

Design/Completion 1991/1995
Tokyo, Japan
Tokyo Teleport Center
1.7 million square feet
Steel, space frame, and long-span structures
Glass, metal
Associate architect: Nissoken Architects and Engineers

1

Tokyo Telecom Center makes a high-tech statement, reinforcing Tokyo's leading edge position in the telecommunications industry. Built on reclaimed land at the edge of Tokyo Bay, the center is the axial focus of the area's emerging telecommunications community.

The twin 24-story tower complex is designed as an abstract form, creating a cube of space within a cube of glass. The two towers are connected at the top by an observation bridge that houses a functional satellite antenna platform; a five-story atrium connects the towers at ground level.

The curtain wall is composed of nested grids. Inside, a cylindrical skylight supported by latticework draws daylight into the cubic atrium. These themes are integrated throughout the building: cube within cube, squares within squares, circles within squares.

2

1 An observation bridge connects the towers
2 Main entry
3 Tokyo Telecom Center's twin towers rise on reclaimed land at the edge of Tokyo Bay
4 Facade with train station in foreground

3

4

Nortel Networks Carling R&D Campus Expansion

Design/Completion 1986/2001
Ottawa, Ontario, Canada
Nortel Networks
1 million+ square feet
Reinforced concrete
Brick and high performance Visionwall glazing system

1

The opening of Lab 10 in 2001 completed a 1-million-square-foot expansion to conclude the 2.4-million-square-foot buildout of Nortel Networks' largest single knowledge campus. The Carling Campus effort between Nortel and HOK began in 1986.

The goal was to design a flexible, innovative "campus of the future" that would attract and keep employees.

The new buildings are designed for autonomy and agility. Each has relatively small floor plates, independent mechanical-electrical systems, separate access systems, and its own sense of identity.

The campus rests on the edge of a greenbelt surrounding Ottawa. While planning expansions on this environmentally sensitive site, designers worked closely with the National Capital Commission's Advisory Committee on Design.

2

3

4

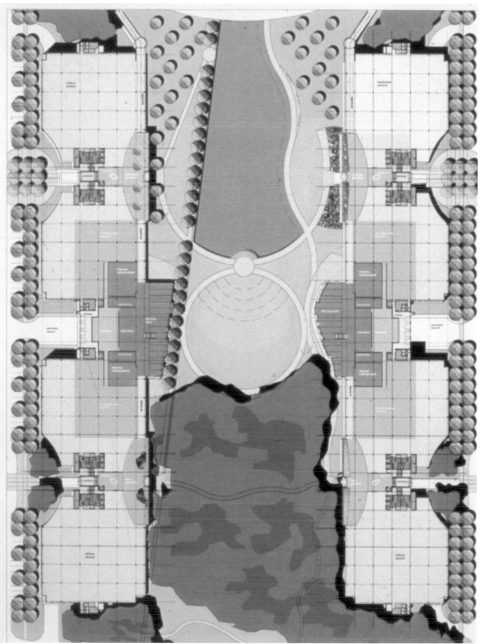

5

6

1 Bright-colored facade adds warmth to cold
  Ottawa winters
2 The three-story buildings stay below tree line
3 Informal meeting room
4 An interior street creates spaces for employees
  to interact
5 Site plan
6 Porthole view of main entry

Boeing Leadership Center

Design/Completion 1996/1999
St. Louis, Missouri, U.S.A.
The Boeing Company
190,000 square feet
Tunnel form concrete, steel, precast concrete structure
Limestone, copper, glass

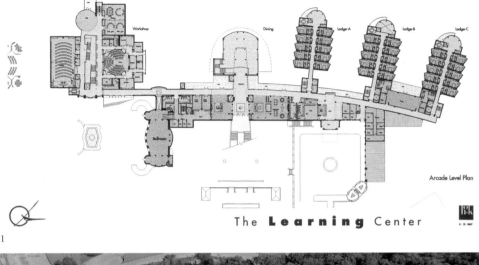

1

The desire to create a collaborative environment that helps people learn to think differently drove the design of Boeing's Leadership Center.

The center sits on the edge of a 286-acre rural site, cantilevered over bluffs overlooking the Mississippi and Missouri Rivers.

The Leadership Center includes residential lodges with private rooms, a workshop building with classrooms, a gourmet dining area, and a theater-style lecture hall.

An existing chateau and its surroundings remain in their original elegant state. This structure and a carriage house, ballroom, and garden pavilions are designed in the French-revival style.

2

1 Arcade level plan
2 Aerial view
3 Site plan
4 North elevation

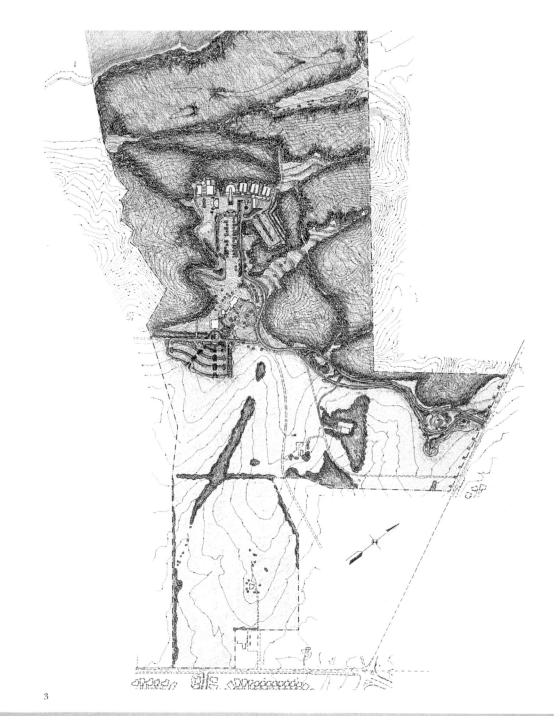

3

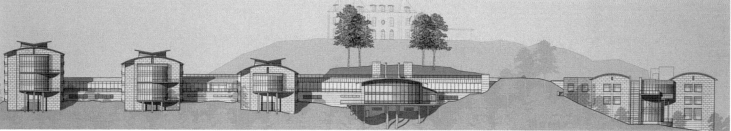

4

5 Residential lodges
6 Meeting room with views to the outside
7 View from bluffs overlooking river
Following page:
   Main dining room

5

6

7

Offices

Queen City Square, Cincinnati, Ohio, U.S.A.

40 Grosvenor Place

Design/Completion 1995/1999
London, England, U.K.
Grosvenor Estate Holdings
350,000 square feet
Cast-in-place and precast concrete structure
Limestone, granite, performance glass, stainless steel, Anolok

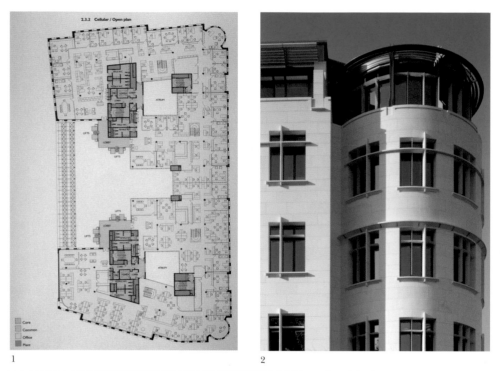

1

2

The objective was to create a socially and environmentally responsible urban workplace.

HOK's design incorporates an integrated mix of community tenant uses surrounding a large atrium or "village within a village." This landscaped atrium provides access to a restaurant, conference center, health club, convenience retail, and a concierge, while offering separate entrances for up to four tenants.

The exterior is a high-performance facade of natural limestone and glass designed to complement the surrounding historic buildings, which include Buckingham Palace.

The British Council for Offices named 40 Grosvenor Place the "Best Commercial Workplace in Britain" in 2001.

3

4

China Resources Building

Design/Completion 1995/1999
Beijing, China
China Resource Building Co., Ltd.
645,000 square feet
Cast-in-place concrete structure
Exterior skin, Blanco Casillo and Verde Lavas granite, high-performance
green tinted glazing and silver metal panels

1 Entry
2 25-story tower
3 Site plan

1

2

The China Resources Building rises above a prestigious site near Tiananmen Square and the ancient imperial Forbidden City. The massing is composed of a 25-story tower, a two-story podium, and three levels of below-grade parking.

The design has a timeless, confident quality that reflects the building's purpose as a corporate headquarters while highlighting its international character.

Strongly reminiscent of both New York and English Art Deco corporate design, the tower's monumental proportions are related in their vocabulary to the neo-gothic Russian 1950s style. This relationship is especially evident in the soaring vertical-tiered detailing of the 330-foot-high facade and tower roofs.

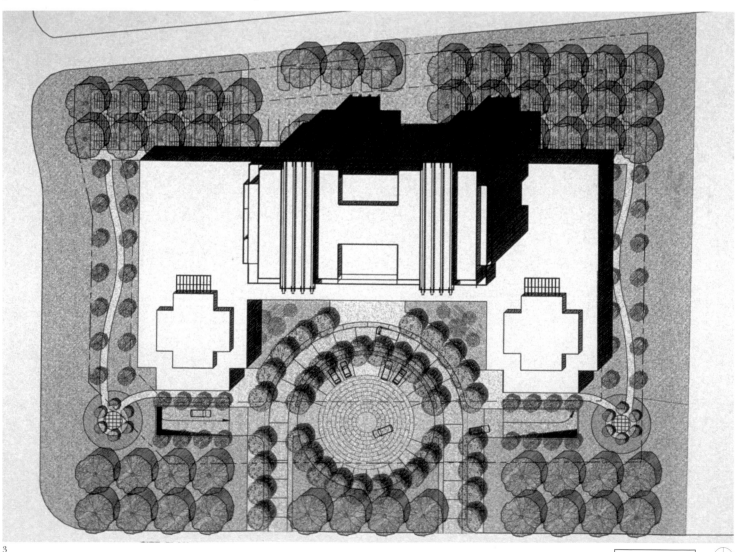

3

0   20ft

Robinson's PCI Bank Tower

Design/Completion 1995/1998
Manila, Philippines
Robinson Land Corporation, Philippines Commercial Industrial Bank
750,000 square feet
Cast-in-place concrete structure
Silver metallic aluminum panels, blue-green glass, unitized curtain wall
system

1   Lower level office plan
2   Metallic aluminum panels and blue-green glass
3   45-story tower

The goal was to establish a landmark headquarters for corporate and banking institutions while providing commercial office space for lease.

Robinson's PCI Bank Tower is located on a prominent site adjacent to the Asian Development Bank in Ortigas Center, Metro Manila. The triangular-shaped site led to the distinctive "Flatiron" configuration of this 45-story tower.

The massing comprises a two-level lobby and banking hall, five stories of podium parking, and 38 stories of office space.

The tower's circular prow provides spectacular views from offices while marking the building's leading edge. A crown creates a landmark skyline image.

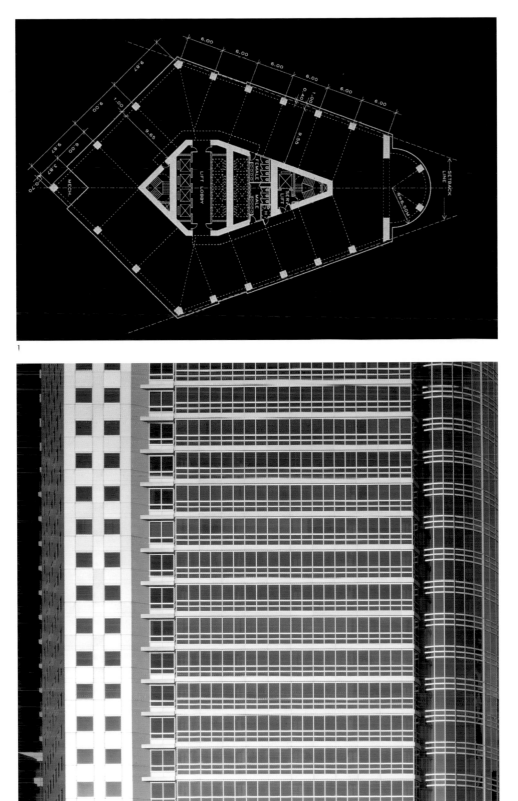

1

2

3

Barranca del Muerto 329

Design/Completion 2001/2003
Mexico City, Mexico
Moisés Farca and Joseph Yelin and Associates
220,000 square feet
Concrete structure
Glass, aluminum, concrete, granite

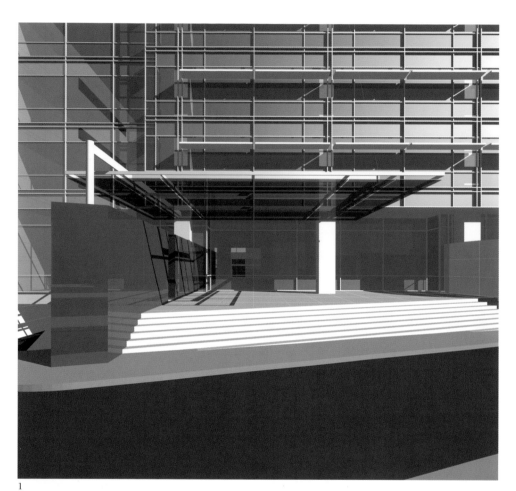

The goal was to create triple A class office space inside an efficient building envelope without sacrificing design.

The project sets a rectangular floor plate onto an irregular site, creating a grandiose triangular entrance plaza that nestles into the surrounding urban fabric.

In order to maximize the built area, the floor plates were extended to the eastern and western edges of the site where two massive concrete walls define the building limits. Between these walls, a series of simple glass planes stretch from one end to the other. Aluminum shading devices and varying mullion depths create an exciting composition of light, shade, and shadow on what is the main building facade.

1   Entry
2   Computer-generated view from front
3   Glass panes and aluminum shading devices create an exciting composition

1

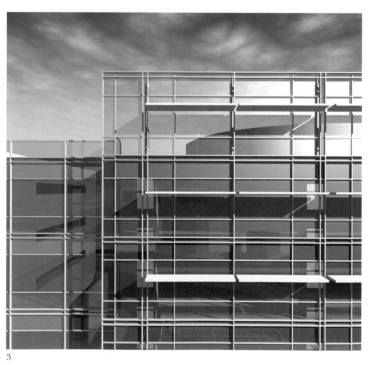

2   3

Lot A

Design/Completion 2000/unbuilt
Sacramento, California, U.S.A.
David Taylor Interests
891,000 square feet
Steel frame
Metal panels and fins, steel truss-work in top screen section, low-E insulated glass, aluminum window system

1

The design for the Lot A mixed-use development proposes a tower that would assume a prominent position on Sacramento's skyline as the city's tallest building.

The tower includes 500,000 square feet of commercial office space, 40,000 square feet of retail space, and parking for 1,000 cars.

Set within California's broad, flat central valley, the tower's design emphasizes verticality and is distinctly modern in character. The building's street elevation is defined by its soaring curtain wall, which tapers gradually from the street to the tower's peak. The building's simple, highly functional floor plates seem to belie the exterior's striking modern image.

1   The building's street elevation is defined by its soaring curtain wall, which tapers gradually from the street to the tower peak
2   Aerial view

2

JTC Summit Headquarters Building

Design/Completion 1996/2000
Jurong East, Singapore
Jurong Town Corporation (JTC), Singapore
600,000 square feet
Reinforced concrete structure with long-span steel atrium roof
Unitized curtain wall of granite, metal and tinted double glazing
Associate architect: Alfred Wong Partnership PTE Ltd., Singapore

1

The 32-story JTC Summit headquarters building for Jurong Town Corporation is a new Singapore landmark. The design of the civil building evokes Singapore's "Garden City" image and position as one of Asia's high-tech leaders.

Designing for openness and transparency helped break down the government's traditional civic face. Street-level arcaded walks and a covered drop-off area engage pedestrians and draw them into a daylight-filled public atrium.

The design features a contemporary interpretation of traditional Singaporean features, such as layered verandas, slatted screens, indoor/outdoor courtyards, and sunshades.

A top-floor viewing gallery and observation deck offer panoramic views of the surrounding high-technology commercial district.

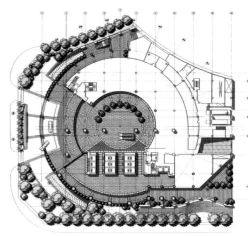

2

3

1   32-story tower
2   Level one plan
3   Daylight-filled atrium
4   Covered drop-off at entrance to public atrium

4

Edificio Malecon

Design/Completion 1996/1999
Buenos Aires, Argentina
Newside, S.A., Buenos Aires, Argentina
125,000 square feet
Cast-in-place concrete frame
Aluminum and glass curtain wall, stone

Edificio Malecon was designed as one of the city's most technologically advanced office buildings. The 12-story tower serves the high end of Buenos Aires' office and commercial space market.

HOK's design presents a "building in the round," with faces in all directions. From the Rio de la Plata to the east and the urban core to the west, it appears as an elegant point tower.

The building geometry, high-performance "skin," and sunscreen systems—coupled with operable windows and an efficient mechanical system—reduce energy costs. The tower rejects unwanted sun and captures the cooling breezes emanating from the nearby river.

The American Institute of Architects (AIA) Committee on the Environment named Edificio Malecon as one of the "Top 10 Green Projects" in 2002.

1

2

1 12-story office tower
2 Sunscreen system
3 Main entry

3

150 California Street

Design/Completion 1997/1999
San Francisco, California, U.S.A.
Equity Office
206,000 square feet
Steel structure
Limestone, granite, glass

Providing unity to a building that straddles two districts was the design goal for this 23-story office tower. Anchoring the corner of Front and California Streets, the building is in the heart of San Francisco's financial district and in the Front-California conservation district.

The design provides architectural unity while accommodating the complex massing requirements. The sense of scale and richness of detail fit the urban fabric.

The California Street elevation is punctuated by a bow front steel and glass window bay that marks the entrance and extends vertically to a glass mechanical penthouse. A glass bar along the west facade acknowledges the transition between districts and accentuates the dramatic verticality.

1   23-story office tower
2   Lobby

Health Care

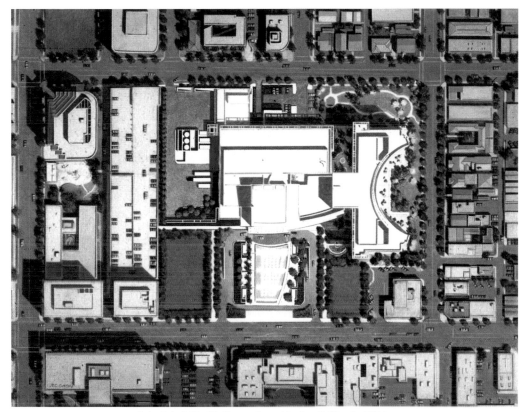

Saint John's Health Center, Santa Monica, California, U.S.A.

Northshore/LIJ Health System

Design/Completion 2001/2002 (facility assessment and master plan)
Long Island, New York, U.S.A.
Northshore/LIJ Health System
1.8 million square feet

1

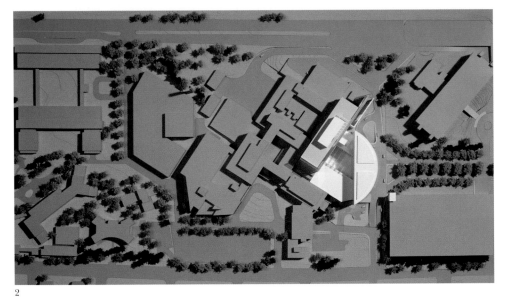

HOK's ongoing work with the Northshore/LIJ Health System in Long Island includes master planning for the LIJ Medical Center campus. The 1.8 million-square-foot master plan encompasses the LIJ Medical Center, Snyders Children's Hospital, and Hillside Hospital.

The plan proposes that a new nursing tower at the campus entrance become the new "front door." The existing bed tower will be reclad and a new entry will lead to the cardiac center. A new lobby and drop-off area will enhance the patient experience. A proposed 50,000-square-foot Emergency Department for the Medical Center will be built over an existing loading dock.

1 Elevation showing nursing tower and front entrance
2 Aerial view of campus model
3 Model showing nursing tower tied into existing bed tower
4 Campus model

2

3

4

LAC + USC Medical Center Replacement Project

Design/Completion 1998/2007
Los Angeles, California, U.S.A.
Los Angeles County
1.5 million square feet
Bracc frame steel structure, seismic base isolation
Precast concrete, sandstone, metal panel, vision and spandrel glass
Associate architect: Lee, Burkhart, Liu (LBL)

1

To meet a growing demand for public healthcare services and to relieve an overburdened, outdated center, the new LAC + USC Medical Center project will replace the nation's largest teaching hospital.

The replacement hospital, consisting of 1.5 million square feet of new construction, will include three major components: a 600-bed inpatient tower, a base isolated diagnostic and treatment building, and an outpatient building.

The new LAC + USC Medical Center will meet current and future medical requirements, acknowledging highly technical medical needs, a growing and changing socioeconomic patient mix, and the need for operational flexibility.

1 Aerial view of replacement hospital model
2 Model showing main entrance
3 Close-up of model
4 Main lobby perspective

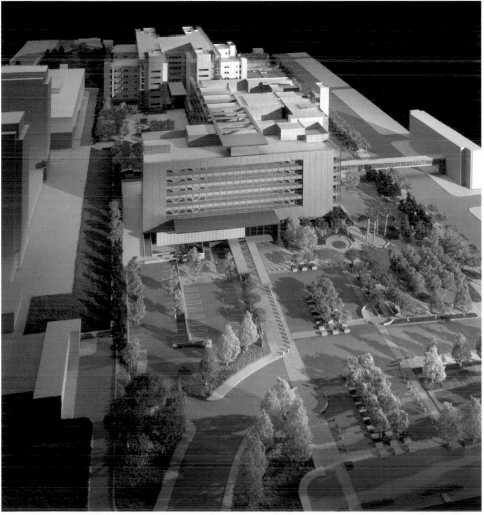

2

3

4

Northwestern Memorial Hospital Facility Replacement and Redevelopment Project

Design/Completion 1991/1999
Chicago, Illinois, U.S.A.
Northwestern Medical Faculty Foundation Group Practice
2 million square feet
Steel and reinforced concrete structure
Precast concrete
Joint venture with Ellerbe Becket and VOA

The facility replacement and redevelopment project for Northwestern Memorial Hospital includes a new inpatient pavilion and ambulatory care facility. The goal was to create a revolution in the delivery of healthcare designed from the patient's point of view.

The design seeks to blend in with the surrounding environment—the Streeterville Neighborhood located one block from Michigan Avenue—yet simultaneously exercise its individuality. While creating one unified structure, the design acknowledges the different ambulatory care and inpatient functions within each pavilion. In each tower, precast concrete and glass have been combined in a stunning composition of richly developed planes and corners, shadow lines, and mullion patterns.

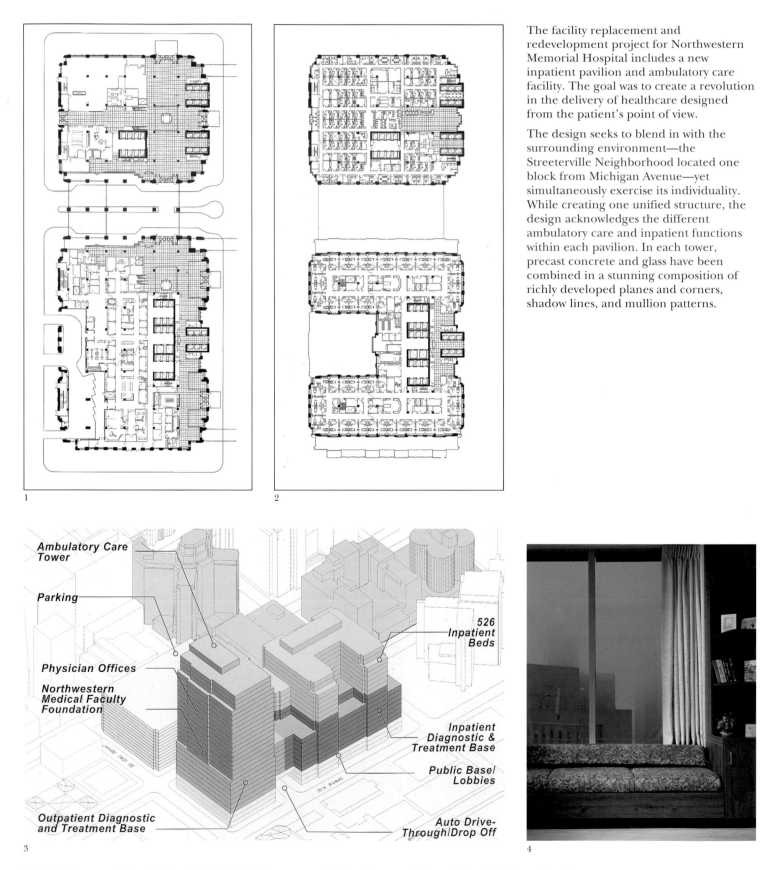

1

2

Ambulatory Care Tower

Parking

Physician Offices

Northwestern Medical Faculty Foundation

Outpatient Diagnostic and Treatment Base

526 Inpatient Beds

Inpatient Diagnostic & Treatment Base

Public Base/ Lobbies

Auto Drive-Through/Drop Off

3

4

1 Ground floor plan
2 Typical physician office tower floor plan (top) and patient bed tower floor plan (bottom)
3 Stacking diagram of overall complex
4 Award-winning pullout bed for visitors in patient rooms
5 Visitors center
6 View of inpatient and ambulatory tower from east

5

6

7 Imaging room
8 Typical patient room

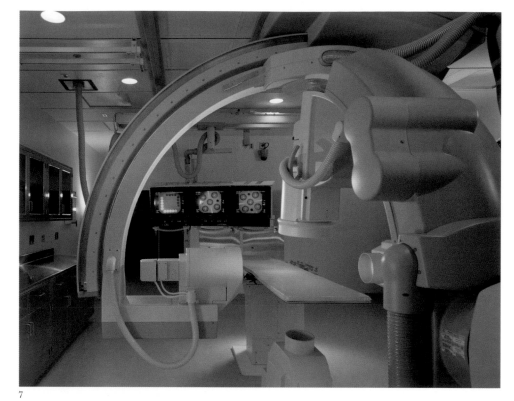

7

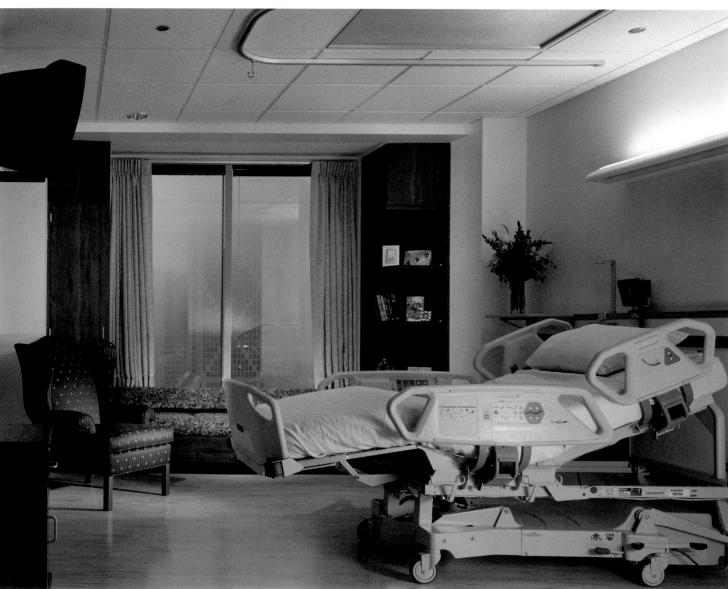

8

184 Northwestern Memorial Hospital Facility Replacement and Redevelopment Project Hellmuth, Obata + Kassabaum

BJC HealthCare Campus Integration Project

Design/Completion 1999/2001
St. Louis, Missouri, U.S.A
BJC HealthCare
Barnes-Jewish Hospital, Washington University School of Medicine
1 million square feet (Phase I)
Steel structure
Precast concrete, metal and glass panels, granite base
Associate architects: Christner, Inc., Cannon

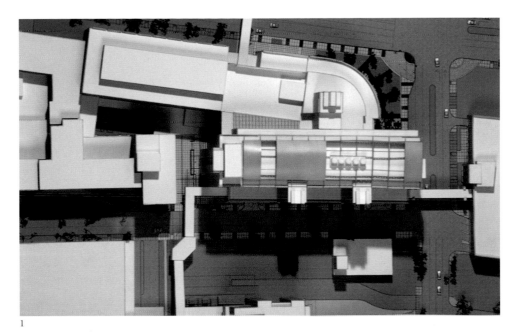

The vision for this healthcare project was to develop a world-class medical campus integrating Barnes Hospital, Jewish Hospital, and Children's Hospital with Washington University School of Medicine. The five-year project includes razing, renovating, and building new facilities on the campus of 7.5 million square feet.

The first phase includes design of the 650,000-square-foot Center for Advanced Medicine and Cancer Center on the north campus with a 1,200-car parking garage. This 14-story tower houses 16 clinical centers of excellence defined by organ and diagnostic group.

Focusing on acute inpatient care, the south campus includes the Charles F. Knight Emergency and Trauma Center, surgery program, laboratory, Children's Hospital entry lobby, and a 750-car parking garage.

1 Aerial view of model showing Center for Advanced Medicine
2 Center for Advanced Medicine from northeast
3 BJC medical campus master plan
4 Atrium

University Health Network

Design/Completion 1997/1998 (master plan), 1997/2001
(R. Fraser Elliott Building), 1997/2003 (Clinical Services Building)
Toronto, Ontario, Canada
University Health Network
4.1 million square feet (master plan for three campuses),
180,000 square feet (R. Fraser Elliott Building),
500,000 square feet (Clinical Services Building)
Poured concrete
Poured concrete, brick and limestone cladding, glazed curtain wall
Joint venture with Urbana Architects Corporation (an HOK worldwide alliance partner)

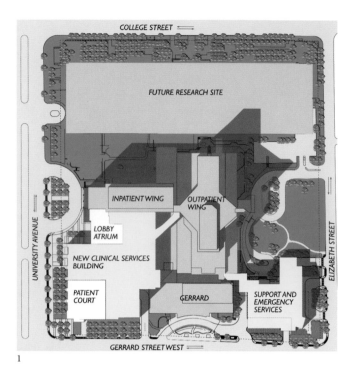

1

Toronto General Campus' R. Fraser Elliott Building represents the first construction project in the University Health Network's five-year master plan to revitalize its aging University Avenue Campus. This six-story support services building houses a new emergency department capable of handling up to 30,000 visits per year, central dock facilities for all three campuses, shelled laboratory space, and executive offices.

The new 12-story Clinical Services Building, located adjacent to the R. Fraser Elliott Building, incorporates the hospital's new imaging facilities, a new surgical floor with 22 operating rooms, and 112 new inpatient rooms on four L-shaped floors. The Patient Court, a four-story glazed therapeutic space located on the inpatient floors, provides a refuge for patients and visitors.

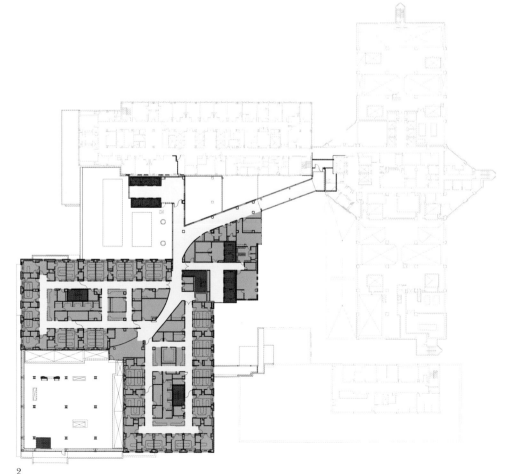

2

3

1 Toronto General campus site plan
2 Inpatient floor plan
3 R. Fraser Elliott Building houses support services and a new emergency department
4 Model showing Toronto General Hospital master plan
5 Computer-generated drawing of The Patient Court, a four-story therapeutic space that provides refuge for patients and visitors
6 Computer-generated drawing of dining area in The Patient Court
7 The Clinical Services Building incorporates new imaging facilities, a surgical floor and inpatient rooms on four floors

4

5

6

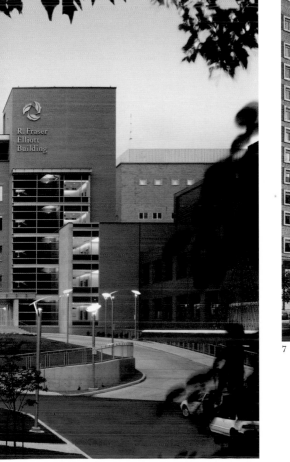

7

Community Hospital of the Monterey Peninsula Pavilions Project

Design/Completion 2001/2006
Monterey, California, U.S.A.
The Community Hospital of the Monterey Peninsula
260,000 square feet (200,000 square feet, new)
(60,000 square feet, renovated)
Reinforced concrete structure
Patterned concrete exterior

1

The Community Hospital of the Monterey Peninsula Pavilions Project consists of new and renovated space, including a new patient bed pavilion and a new diagnostic and treatment pavilion.

The expansion integrates the new facilities into an environmentally sensitive area while maintaining the integrity, scale, and character of the original facility, which was designed by Edward Durell Stone.

Low, striking rooflines, sweeping views to the Pacific Ocean and Monterey Pine forests, and numerous naturally lit public spaces all contribute to a calm, healing environment.

3

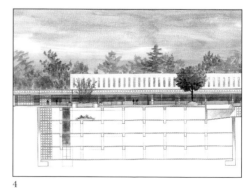

2

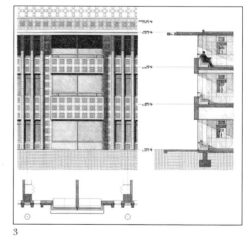

4

1   Campus courtyard
2   Aerial view of model showing site
3   Typical bay window detail
4   Elevation showing parking below grade

Planning

Troia Resort Community, Setubal, Portugal

West Kowloon Waterfront

Design/Completion 2001/2001 (design competition)
Hong Kong, China
Hong Kong Government
100 acres
Associates: City Planning Consultants Ltd., Economics Research Associates

The West Kowloon Waterfront master plan introduces new life into Hong Kong's Victoria Harbour. The project creates a mixed-use urban center and international tourist destination on reclaimed land north of Hong Kong Island.

Unified by a premier waterfront promenade and monorail system, this exciting combination of recreation, commercial, and tourist amenities reinforces Hong Kong as the "City of Life."

The plan forms five distinct yet connected nodes along Victoria Harbour. Nodes include an arts and cultural district, convention center, island park, stadium, and wholesale market. Each component celebrates both Hong Kong's history and its new cultural life.

1 Site plan
2 Aerial rendering

1

2

Fort Bonifacio Master Plan

Design/Completion 1995/1996 (master plan)
Manila, Philippines
Fort Bonifacio Development Corporation
1,100 acres

Envisioned as the centerpiece for a new Manila that will be at the forefront of Asian planning and urban design, Fort Bonifacio will ultimately house a daytime population of more than one million people and accommodate some 250,000 full-time residents.

This new city is rising on a 1,100-acre site that once housed a former Philippine Army base. The master plan provides a broad vision and detailed planning, urban design, and landscape guidelines for more than 100 million square feet of public, residential, commercial, and mixed-use space.

The creation of neighborhoods and a distinct "character of place" was interwoven with strategies for transportation, open spaces, infrastructure, public facilities, and environmentally sensitive solid waste disposal and water use. This integrated planning approach will reduce the environmental impact of the development, thereby conserving land and infrastructure and energy resources while maintaining good air quality.

The vision established by HOK is now being carried forward by several entities working to establish a new benchmark for a high-quality urban environment in Asia.

1 Site plan
2 Perspective of new urban area
3 Aerial view of model

Stella Maris Monastery Master Plan

Design/Completion 1999/to be determined
Haifa, Israel
Discalced Carmelite Order
50 acres

The Stella Maris Monastery is on the western-most promontory of Mount Carmel, overlooking the Mediterranean Sea. The monastery commands a spectacular panorama of Haifa Bay and the sea below.

The Carmelite Fathers commissioned HOK to create a master development plan that would maintain the sanctity of the monastery and religious zone.

The monastery grounds will feature a processional colonnade with landscaped prayer gardens, a 1,000-person amphitheater, a restored Via Dolorosa, and inspirational artwork.

Outside the religious zone, the mixed-use development will include residential and commercial space, a tourist-oriented village, subterranean parking, a hotel, and a public park and gardens.

1 Site plan showing program elements
2 Rendering of public playground
3 Rendering of mixed-use development

שימושי קרקע Land Use	שטח בניה Built Area	כמות Capacity	מספר קומות Height	גודל היחידה Unit Size
בתי מגורים מדורגים Terraced Apartments	6500 sm	50 units	2 stories	130 sm ave.
איזור מגורים Residential	40,560 sm	312 units	4-5 stories 9 stories	130 sm ave.
כפר נופש תיירותי Tourist Village Apartments	5000 sm	100 units	2-3 stories	100 sm ea.
דיורית לגיל הזהב Elder Care Apartments	6200 sm	100 units	5 stories	50 sm ea.
מבני דת Religious Buildings	2050 sm	-	1-2 stories	-
מסחר Commercial	2500 sm	-	1 story/arcade	-
מרכז מסחרי תיירותי Tourist Commercial	4000 sm	-	1 story	-
מלון נופש Resort Hotel	4400 sm	50 rooms	1 story villas 2-3 story villas	-
חניון פתוח Surface Parking	1500 sm	75 cars 12 buses	-	-
חניון תת קרקעי Parking Structure	34,200 sm	900 cars 20 buses	2 levels	-

Stella Maris
Our Lady of Mount Carmel
Discalced Carmelite Order
Haifa, Israel

Program Elements
פרוגרמה

פרוייקט סטלה מאריס
חיפה, ישראל

1

2

3

Dubai Marina

Design/Completion 2000/2003 (Phase I, Municipal Landscape Design)
Dubai, United Arab Emirates
Emaar Properties, PJSC
28 acres (Phase I)
Joint venture with Urbana Architects Corporation
(an HOK worldwide alliance partner)

Carved along a 2-mile stretch of Arabian Gulf shoreline, Dubai Marina is a mixed-use canal-city inspired by the Venetian tradition. Phase I of the master plan, which ultimately will house as many as 100,000 expatriate workers, ties together a complex system of dual podium structures and provides an elevated rooftop garden for six residential towers and several villas.

In front of the podium structure, a new marina keywall provides an area for a pedestrian and bicycle promenade along a retail colonnade. The team is also designing the streetscape, plaza areas, and a small urban park.

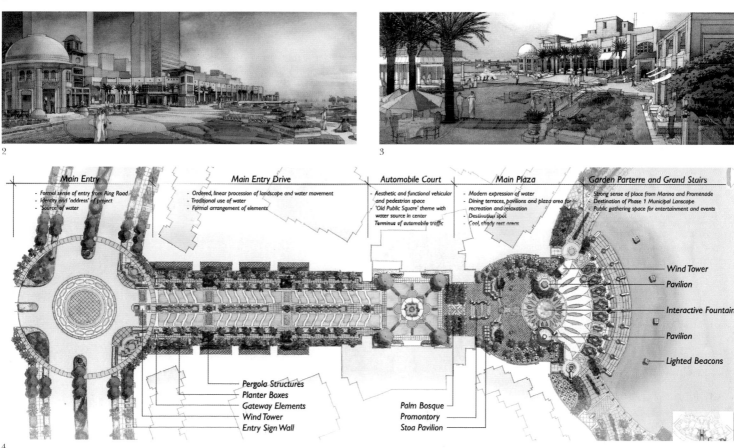

1   Promenade along cove
2   Main plaza facing shoreline
3   Main plaza
4   Main entry plan

Downtown St. Louis Chouteau Lake District and Ballpark Village

Design/Completion 1999/2000 (Chouteau Lake District)
St. Louis, Missouri, U.S.A.
McCormack Baron Associates, Inc.
195 acres

Design/Completion 1999/2001 (Ballpark Village)
St. Louis, Missouri, U.S.A.
St. Louis Cardinals
1,294,000 square feet

The Chouteau Lake District is a 195-acre planned development for a series of distinct neighborhoods and new downtown housing anchored by beautiful public spaces and a prominent water feature. The plan centers around the redevelopment of Chouteau Lake, the jewel of the early village of St. Louis.

The new District encompasses the proposed St. Louis baseball park and the adjacent "Ballpark Village," which features residential, office, and retail development designed to bring year-round vibrancy to the urban landscape.

Together, these projects will catalyze development, become important new pieces of the city fabric, and reconnect city neighborhoods with a rejuvenated downtown.

1 Chouteau Lake District master plan
2 Ballpark Village adjacent to new stadium

1

2

Confluence Greenway

Design/Completion 1999/2010 (conceptual master plan)
Metropolitan St. Louis, Missouri and Illinois, U.S.A.
Confluence Greenway
200-square miles

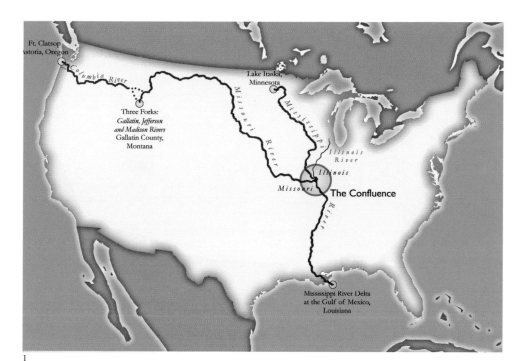

1

This master plan creates a perpetually sustainable 40-mile riverside park in Missouri and Illinois.

The plan encompasses 200 square miles of natural, agricultural, and developed land, and extends from the Gateway Arch in downtown St. Louis to the Mississippi River's confluences with the Missouri and Illinois Rivers. Linear parks, pedestrian and bicycle trails, conservation areas, and interpretive centers will provide a variety of recreational and educational experiences.

The master plan highlights the opportunity for linking the Confluence Greenway to a growing national corridor network, including American Discovery Trail, the Lewis and Clark National Historic Trail, the Great River Road, and Route 66.

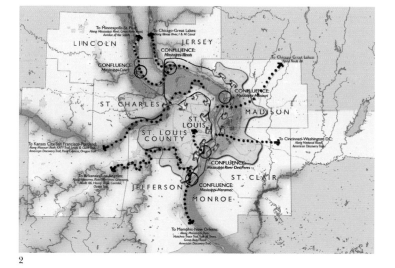

2

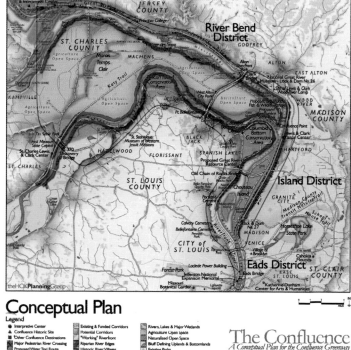

Conceptual Plan

The Confluence
A Conceptual Plan for the Confluence Greenway

3

1 Map showing Mississippi and Missouri rivers as national river sources
2 Map showing meeting of the rivers at center of the region
3 Conceptual plan

New Town Center in Research Triangle Park

Design/Completion 2000/2000 (master plan, design guidelines, architectural prototypes)
Raleigh-Durham, North Carolina, U.S.A.
Craig Davis Properties
25 acres

The master plan for this new 25-acre town center incorporates commercial, retail, residential, hospitality, and civic with a focus on a bus transfer station and future rail station.

Building types were developed that allow ground floor retail and commercial use with the flexibility of office or residential uses on the upper floors.

The streets are hierarchical and the center is clearly defined. In the tradition of town-making, streets are the most active public spaces.

The plan creates an opportunity for this community to test its new transit-oriented development ordinance.

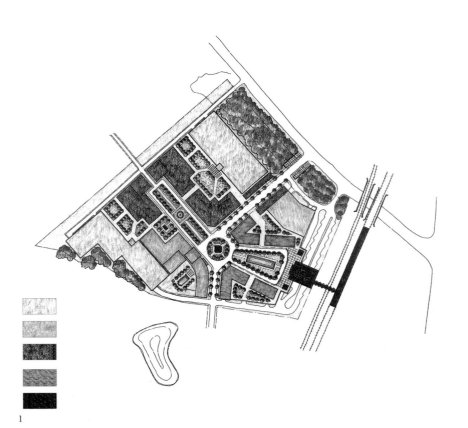

1

1   Master plan for 25-acre town center
2   Aerial view of new town center

2

Esquire Plaza

Design/Completion 1996/2000
Sacramento, California, U.S.A.
Lankford & Taylor
75 acres

1

2

Located at the end of Sacramento's "K" Street Mall, this urban plaza enhances a new 23-story office tower at the corner of 13th and "K" Streets. It is also designed to complement the renovation of two existing art deco theaters into a new IMAX theater and the reconfiguration of 13th Street as a tree-lined pedestrian and vehicular promenade.

The plaza, which is developed around a sculptural fountain, creates a dynamic space that helps reinvigorate a portion of downtown Sacramento that had lost its urban vitality.

1   Art along promenade
2   Urban plaza with sculptural fountain
3   Site plan

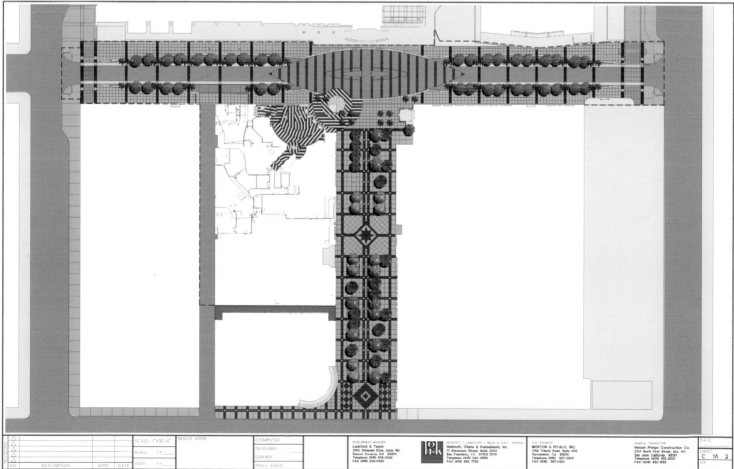

3

Police and Firefighter Memorial Plaza

Design/Completion 2000
Clayton, Missouri, U.S.A.
St. Louis County
14,000 square feet

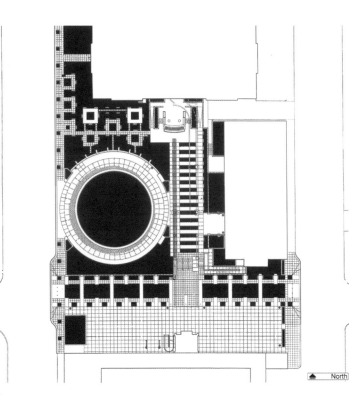

The master plan for the St. Louis County Government Campus in Clayton, Missouri included the design of the Police and Firefighter Memorial Plaza and monuments in a new 14,000-square-foot public park.

In addition to developing an appropriate setting for the Memorial, design goals included creating an environment for a safe, aesthetically pleasing urban park. The plaza and ring meadow provide a gathering space for people using the adjacent government complex and for Clayton's residents, employees, and visitors.

1　Base plan
2　Overall view of park with Memorial Plaza and monuments

Housing

One McKinley, Manila, Philippines

Sun City Machida

Design/Completion 1995/2000
Tokyo, Japan
Half Century More Co., Ltd.
230,000 square feet
Steel and concrete structure
Tile exterior, stone and wood interior
Architect of record: JDC Co., Ltd.
Design architects: HOK, Inc.; Office of Dennis Cope/Architect
Interior designers: Hirsch-Bedner Associates (Independent Living Building);
Graeber, Simmons & Cowan (Assisted/Skilled Nursing Building)

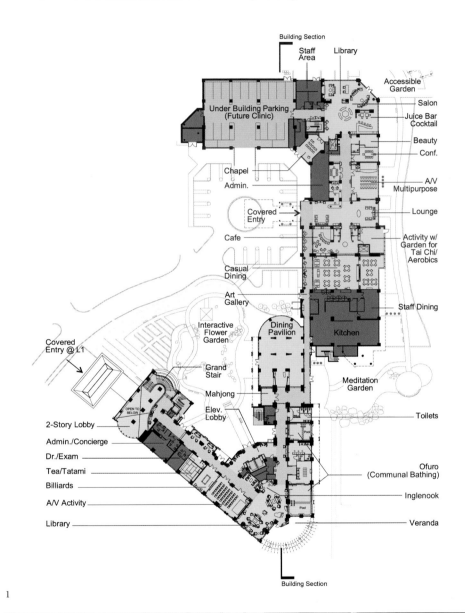

A blending of traditional Japanese culture and "western" senior lifestyle amenities was the design goal for this thriving community for Japanese elderly ranging in age from 65 to 90 and beyond.

A central courtyard, formed through the siting of the buildings, is shared by all residents. A common public level gives all residents a linked, integrated and community-shared parade of diverse amenities and services. Constant contact with and awareness of nature were design concepts that have enriched the lives of all residents, regardless of their degree of frailty. The collaboration that resulted made it possible for an emergence of eastern and western aesthetics, and introduces new care-giving philosophies.

Honored with a "Gold Award" in the Best of Seniors Housing Design Awards 2002 competition, the facility is 100 percent occupied.

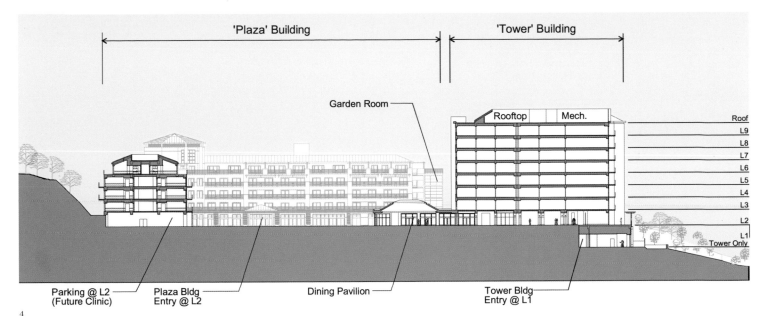

'Plaza' Building   'Tower' Building

Garden Room

Rooftop | Mech.

Roof
L9
L8
L7
L6
L5
L4
L3
L2
L1
Tower Only

Parking @ L2 (Future Clinic) — Plaza Bldg Entry @ L2 — Dining Pavilion — Tower Bldg Entry @ L1

4

5

7

6

1   Level two floor plan
2   Light-filled corridor
3   Independent living facility lobby
4   Community section
5   Lounge area
6   Typical bedroom
7   Covered entry

Embassy House Phase II Residential Complex

Design/Completion 1997/2002
Beijing, China
Half Century More Co. Ltd., Hines
Reinforced concrete structure
Curtain wall, tinted vision glass spandrel glazing and metal panels

1 Tower rendering

Located in the prestigious Second Embassy District of Beijing, this 32-story tower meets the needs of the primarily expatriate residential market.

To fit the site's geometry, the apartment tower forms a trapezoid with rounded corners, housing the building's end units. At the core, a rectangular form intersects the trapezoid structure to align with the predominant city grid and provide the building's central apartment layouts.

The floor plan provides each resident with southern, eastern, or western light. The design eliminates exclusively northern exposures for any apartments and minimizes the impact of shadows on the office and residential buildings to the north.

1

Huaqiang Plaza

Design/Completion 2002/2004
Shenzhen, China
Huaqiang Development Co. Ltd.
2 million square-foot mixed-use development, 600,000 square feet
(residential), 750,000 square feet (retail), 280,000 square feet (hotel),
370,000 square feet (office)
Reinforced concrete frame
Unitized double-glazed curtain wall (tower), interactive graphic display
(residential), tile finish (residential)

1

2

The master plan for Huaqiang Plaza
integrates three residential towers, a
high-rise office and hotel tower, and a
commercial podium. This new urban
landmark will become a model for future
developments in Shenzhen City.

The residential space is distributed across
three towers resting on the western edge of
the commercial podium. The towers create
a well-defined residential area while
maximizing views of landscaped space
below.

Rotating the towers 45 degrees to the south
allows more units to enjoy views to the
south and southwest while providing
necessary privacy.

1 Level five floor plan
2 Computer-generated aerial
3 Unit plan

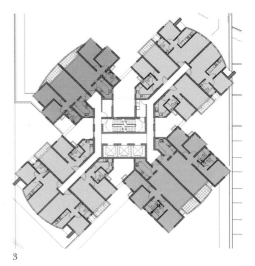

3

West India Quay Tower

Design/Completion 2000/2004
London, England, U.K.
West India Quay Development Co. (Eastern) Ltd. (consists of Manhattan
Loft Corporation Ltd. and Marylebone Warwick and Balfour)
653,724 square feet
Post-tensioned concrete structure with glazed facade and stainless steel
details
Glass cladding with terracotta panels

1

This 500-unit hotel and apartment tower is at West India Quay, adjacent to the Canary Wharf Estate in London's Docklands.

The tight urban site, dual-use cores, complex ground conditions, and challenging occupancy requirements present many opportunities. The design features an elegant 36-story faceted facade facing its neighbors of the South Canary Wharf and a terracotta plinth to the north to marry into the old warehouse.

The use of shading on the facade significantly enhances the tower's energy performance. Shear walls are nearly eliminated by the strategic placement of stairs and cores.

1 Computer-generated rendering of tower and site
2 Upper level floor plan

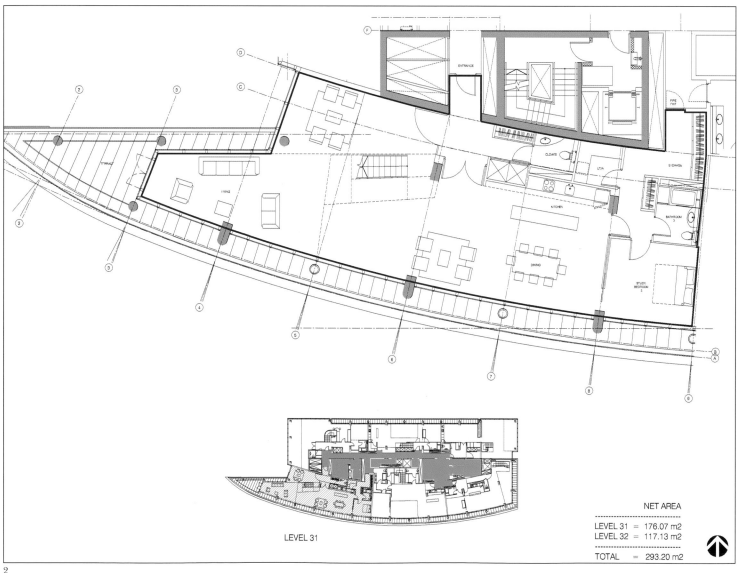

LEVEL 31

NET AREA

LEVEL 31 = 176.07 m2
LEVEL 32 = 117.13 m2

TOTAL   = 293.20 m2

2

Harbour View Estates at CityPlace

Design/Completion 2002/2004
Toronto, Ontario, Canada
Concord Adex Development Corporation
1,160,500 square feet
Reinforced concrete structure
Aluminum mullions and panels, tinted glass
Associate architect: Urbana Architects Corporation
(an HOK worldwide alliance partner)

Harbour View Estates is comprised of two high-rise condominium towers and a mid-rise condominium building. The development represents Phase IV of downtown Toronto's 23-acre, multi-phased CityPlace redevelopment of a former "Railway Lands" site.

Phase I of Harbour View Estates consists of a 40-story tower accommodating 417 suites, a seven-story, 102-unit loft-style condominium building, and a two-story retail and daycare facility over three levels of underground parking.

Phase II consists of a 49-story tower with 522 suites over a three-level underground parking structure.

1   Model of Phase I

1

Dubai Marina Resort, Condominium and Rental Residential

Design/Completion 2000/2003
Dubai, United Arab Emirates
Emaar Properties PJSC
Phase I Architecture 3,740,000 square feet, Master Plan Inclusive
1,200 acres
Reinforced concrete structure
Precast concrete, aluminum mullions and panes, curtain wall, tinted glass
Joint venture with Urbana Architects Corporation (an HOK worldwide alliance partner)

1

Carved along a 2-mile stretch of Arabian Gulf shoreline, Dubai Marina is a mixed-use canal-city inspired by the Venetian tradition. The development is planned to accommodate more than 120,000 people in mid-to-high-luxury condominium towers and villas perched atop a dynamic waterfront-retail promenade.

Phase I includes six residential towers and villas totaling over 1,000 units, connected by a spectacular network of rooftop gardens. Interior layouts combine large living and dining room areas, separate bedroom wings, and traditional spaces that recognize the resort-styled community's Islamic context.

HOK master planned Dubai Marina and is providing Phase I architecture, retail programming, and landscape design.

2

3

4

1   Model of Phase I
2   Typical three-bedroom plan
3   Master site plan
4   Rendering of promenade along shoreline

Conservation/Preservation

Natural History Museum, London, England, U.K.

St. Louis Union Station

Design/Completion 1981/1985
St. Louis, Missouri, U.S.A.
The Rouse Company/St. Louis Station Associates
822,00 square feet
Headhouse: existing Bedford limestone structure, existing wood beams reinforced with steel flitch plates
Hotel: existing train shed is cast-in-place post-tension concrete
Retail: under train shed is cast-in-place concrete waffle-slab
Ballrooms: steel joists with steel beams and columns
Headhouse and midway: Bedford limestone
New hotel: lightweight insulated wall panels and glass

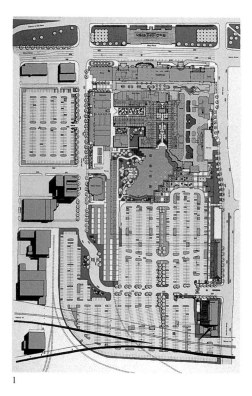

1

2

3

When it opened in 1894, St. Louis Union Station was the world's largest single-level passenger train terminal. Today it is listed on the National Historic Register.

The conversion of historic St. Louis Union Station into a 35-acre mixed-use development represents the largest preservation project in the city's history and one of the largest rehabilitation projects in the U.S., involving a combination of new construction and meticulous historic restoration.

Nostalgia blends with modern conveniences in the barrel-vaulted grand hall with its gold leaf, stenciling, and stained glass; the L-shaped retail "street" under the steel and glass canopy of the train shed roof; and the luxury hotel and meeting rooms.

4

1 Site plan
2 Night view of headhouse and clock tower
3 Detail of restored Grand Hall
4 Looking north along the "retail street" under the train shed roof
Opposite:
 Restored barrel-vaulted Grand Hall

Foreign & Commonwealth Office, Whitehall

Design/Completion 1980/1997
London, England, U.K.
Foreign & Commonwealth Office
1,000,000 square feet
Load-bearing masonry structure
Stone, slate, decorative leadwork (exterior); cast iron, wrought iron, decorative plaster, painted finishes and murals, joinery, marble, ceramics (interior)

Retaining the character of the original 1870s Victorian construction while creating one of the U.K.'s most technologically advanced buildings was the challenge for the Foreign & Commonwealth Office refurbishment. A phased program spanning 17 years allowed occupants to remain on site and operations to continue without interruption.

The refurbishment plan recognizes the clear distinction between the Office's political departments, which respond to world events, and its support services, which have predetermined and ongoing technical requirements. The design creates accommodation efficiencies that enable all departments to consolidate operations onto a single site.

Conservation elements included identifying the building's historically and architecturally significant areas, and working with English Heritage and specialist conservators to restore them to their original appearance. Use of original materials, colors, and building techniques retains the historic character and harmonizes new and old elements.

The practice earned the prestigious Europa Nostra Medal of Honour for the meticulous detailing work.

1 Facade
2 Staircase and ceiling detail
3 Atrium
4 Locarno suite conference room

5   Grand reception room
6   Secretary of State's office

5

6

Museums

John and Mable Ringling Museum of Art, Sarasota, Florida

National Air and Space Museum

Design/Completion 1971/1976
Washington, D.C., U.S.A.
Smithsonian Institution
630,000 square feet
Structural steel and poured-in-place concrete structure
Light steel frame, marble panels

Creating a suitable complement to its neighbors, which include the National Gallery of Art, was the main design consideration for the National Air and Space Museum (NASM), which celebrates the United States' remarkable achievements in flight.

The museum is formed from simple design elements: four geometric blocks clad in marble matching the exterior of the National Gallery alternate with three glass-enclosed exhibit bays. These glass bays provide the dominant focus, creating what *Newsweek* magazine described as "an outdoor spaciousness and freedom totally unexpected in a building so packed with displays."

Regarded as the world's most-visited museum, the National Air and Space Museum hosts approximately 10 million visitors each year.

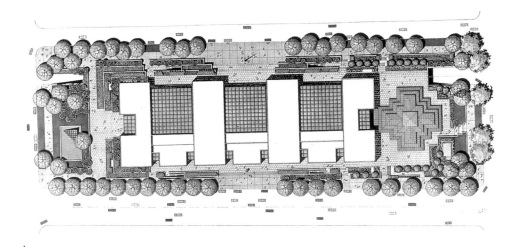

1

2

3

4

National Air and Space Museum
Steven F. Udvar-Hazy Center

Design/Completion 1995/2003
Chantilly, Virginia, U.S.A.
Smithsonian Institution
711,000 square feet
Exposed structural trusses
Metal panels, ceramic tile panels, low-E glass, membrane roofing system

The Smithsonian Institution's National Air and Space Museum Steven F. Udvar-Hazy Center is an extension of the original National Air and Space Museum, designed by HOK in the 1970s.

The site, located next to Dulles Airport, permits large air and spacecraft exhibition pieces to fly directly to the museum. The facility includes exhibition areas, a theater, an observation tower, and a large restoration and preservation hangar.

The hangar will be the Museum's sole facility for a growing collection of historical artifacts. The environmental and energy conservation systems, which include thermal storage, will set a new standard of artifact preservation.

1 Main entrance
2 Section
3 Main exhibit hangar

1

2

3

Japanese American National Museum
Phase II Pavilion

Design/Completion 1992/1997
Los Angeles, California, U.S.A.
138,000 square feet
Concentric steel-braced frame structure
Granite, sandstone, glass, stainless steel, natural wood
Associate architect: O'Leary-Terasawa Partner

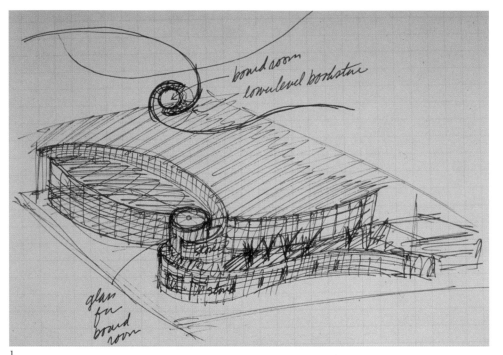

Designed to respect and honor its past while looking to the future, the Pavilion establishes a dialogue with the existing historic building, the former Nishi Hongwanji Buddhist Temple, the Museum's largest artifact.

Conceived as a national resource center with regional partnerships around the world, the facility enables visitors to access a wealth of materials from within the structure or electronically from around the globe. The collection is rich and diverse, ranging from oral histories, photographs, and documents to three-dimensional objects, works of art, and moving images.

1   Conceptual drawing
2   First level floor plan
3   Glass outer wall surrounds central hall
4   Central hall
5   Outdoor plaza
6   National resource center
7   Main entrance

1

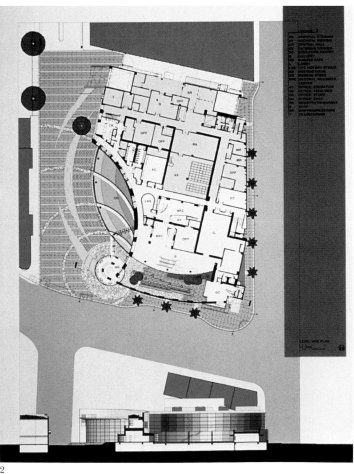

2   3

4

5

6

7

Missouri Historical Society Expansion and Renovation

Design/Completion 1997/1999
St. Louis, Missouri, U.S.A.
Missouri Historical Society
129,000 square feet
Steel and concrete structure
Precast concrete and low-E insulating glass curtain wall systems,
copper wall panels

The primary design considerations for this museum addition were to connect the natural setting of St. Louis' Forest Park with the urban edge along a city street, and to change the public's perception of the building from an inaccessible monument to an active center of community life.

The design maintains the museum's original north-south axis and breaks the building down into discrete zones projecting south into the park.

The addition embraces the use of technology to accomplish the client's goals for environmentally friendly design. Building systems were designed to maximize natural light, ventilation, and energy efficiency.

1   Main entrance
2   Lobby joining expansion with existing museum

Abraham Lincoln Presidential Library & Museum

Design/Completion 1999/2002 (library) 2004 (museum)
Springfield, Illinois, U.S.A.
CDB, Illinois/State of Illinois, Illinois Historic Preservation Agency
99,600 square feet (library) 120,000 square feet (museum)
Steel structure
Limestone

The desire to create a comprehensive public experience focused on the life of the 16th U.S. president is embodied in this new Abraham Lincoln Presidential Library & Museum. The design creates a new Springfield landmark.

The facility will provide a new state-of-the-art library to house the Illinois State Historical Library's existing artifacts and documents.

The museum creates an interactive visitor experience for both children and adults using the latest multimedia technology.

Together, the library and museum create a comprehensive environment in which visitors can learn about and experience the life of Lincoln.

1   Rendering of museum lobby
2   Rendering of museum and library
3   First level floor plan, museum
4   Model of site plan

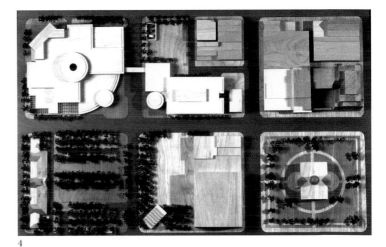

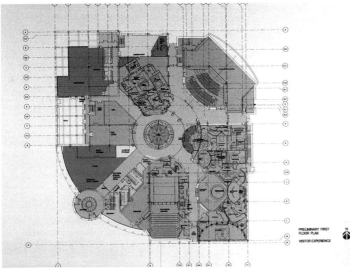

Astronauts Memorial Foundation, Center for Space Education

Design/Completion 1990/1995
Kennedy Space Center, Florida, U.S.A.
Astronauts Memorial Foundation, The Center for Space Education
44,000 square feet
Steel structure
Metal and glass

Housing the educational, information distribution, and archival activities of the National Aeronautics and Space Administration (NASA), the Astronauts Memorial is a resource for the history of the U.S. space program.

The design is educationally and environmentally responsive while also relating to the Space Mirror and the collection of neighboring metal buildings that constitute "Spaceport USA."

The design integrates the structure, service, and enclosure systems to highlight an understanding of the new Astronauts Memorial while relating to the hardware of space exploration. The double structure, which is expressed by the wind bracing, creates a transverse distribution zone fed from horizontal chases in the high-bay spaces. The open display of structural, mechanical, and lighting elements becomes a learning tool. The enclosure system identifies each building element while creating a unified expression of ribbed, perforated, striated, and smooth metal panels.

A translucent roof and clerestory windows provide natural lighting to central corridors. The eastern office exposure features glass sunshades, while the western classrooms use a translucent wall for solar control.

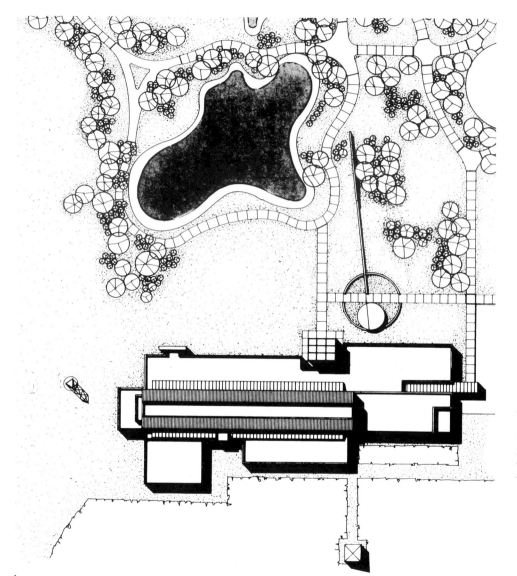

1

2

1   Site plan
2   Side entry
3   Main entry
4   Fenestration detail

3

4

Hellmuth, Obata + Kassabaum **Astronauts Memorial Foundation, Center for Space Education 223**

Darwin Centre

Design/Completion 1998/2002
London, England, U.K.
Natural History Museum
120,000 square feet
Steel frame
Terracotta panels, glass solar wall, stainless steel, ETFE roof

Phase I of the Darwin Centre at the Natural History Museum uses contemporary detailing to recreate the historic tradition of "architecture parlante," in which a building's external appearance describes what happens inside.

The zoomorphic brackets of the solar wall, the changing appearance created by the sun-tracking metal louvers, and the triple-skin, caterpillar-like inflated roof refer directly to the contents of the building, which will house more than one million biological specimens preserved in spirit.

1   Atrium, view from top floor at dusk
2   West elevation
3   Zoomorphic brackets support glass solar wall

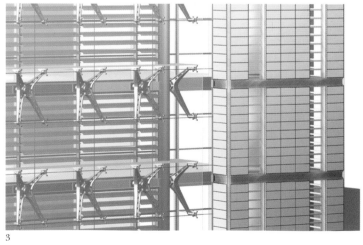

Worship

B'nai Amoona, St. Louis County, Missouri, U.S.A.

The Priory Chapel

Design/Completion 1959/1962
St. Louis, Missouri, U.S.A.
The Benedictines of St. Louis
25,500 square feet
Poured-in-place concrete structure
Fiberglass (smoke-gray on the exterior, white on the interior)

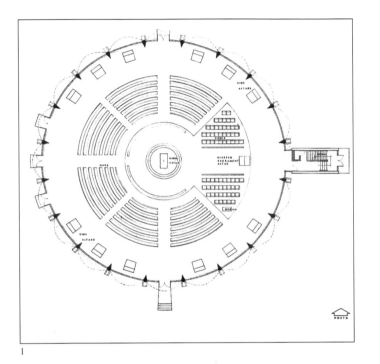

1

2

Although their tradition was largely rooted in Gothic architecture, the Benedictines of St. Louis wanted to bring a fresh approach to their new home. The Priory Chapel was to be "living" architecture, to reflect the methods, style, and materials of the time in which it was built.

The chapel was designed to accommodate more than 600 people and to create a strong sense of participation among the congregation. Rows of pews encircle the central high altar to draw the entire congregation closer to the officiating priest.

The external shapes consist of three ascending concentric rings of parabolic arches. The first layer of arches, approximately 22 feet high, houses 20 small monastic chapels. An intermediate layer brings light into the nave of the church, and a bell tower with a lantern above the central altar crowns the chapel.

The arches enfold parabolic windows constructed of a double layer of fiberglass, smoke-gray on the exterior and white on the interior. Though they appear black from the outside, the windows admit a soft white glow into the church during the day.

1 Main floor plan
2 View of illuminated ceiling
3 Detail showing bell tower
4 View of central high altar
5 Southeast elevation

St. Barnabas Church

Design/Completion 1993/1995
Dulwich, England, U.K.
St. Barnabas Church
10,000 square feet
Brick masonry structure
Glass spire, beech slatted ceiling, slate and terra cotta flooring, brick piers

Influencing the design of this suburban London church was the parish's desire to create a welcoming, functional, adaptable symbol of Christian witness in the community. The parish's 100-year-old Victorian church had been destroyed by fire. Parish leaders developed a program for the new church combining expressive aspiration and technical requirements.

The landmark building ultimately constructed is significantly different than early designs with one exception: the glass spire. The spire's transparent nature reinforces the ancient use of light as a symbol of divine presence, a theme developed throughout the church interior.

The roof's main structure draws in light from above through paired beams, admitting a soft and diffuse light that contrasts with the direct light from windows to the east and west. Eight massive brick piers enclose the space, recalling the old church building while symbolizing the new church and its people—rising up from the earth to light.

1   Main entry
2   Night view of illuminated church
3   Typical floor plan
4   Sanctuary
5   Interior view showing abundance of natural light

1

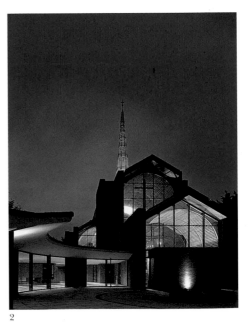

2

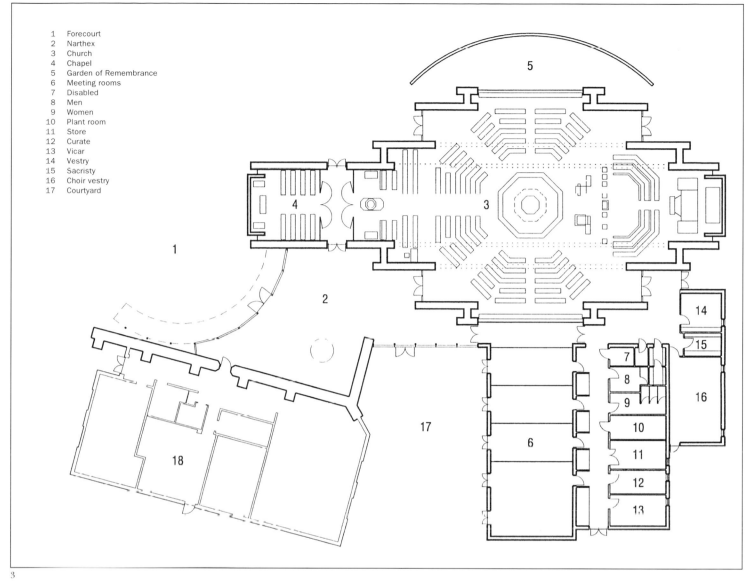

1 Forecourt
2 Narthex
3 Church
4 Chapel
5 Garden of Remembrance
6 Meeting rooms
7 Disabled
8 Men
9 Women
10 Plant room
11 Store
12 Curate
13 Vicar
14 Vestry
15 Sacristy
16 Choir vestry
17 Courtyard

3

4

5

Our Lady of the Snows National Shrine

Design/Completion 1987/1991
Belleville, Illinois, U.S.A.
The Missionary Oblates of Mary Immaculate
18,000 square feet
Concrete and steel structure
Architectural concrete, aluminum, glass,
Kalwal, exterior plaster system

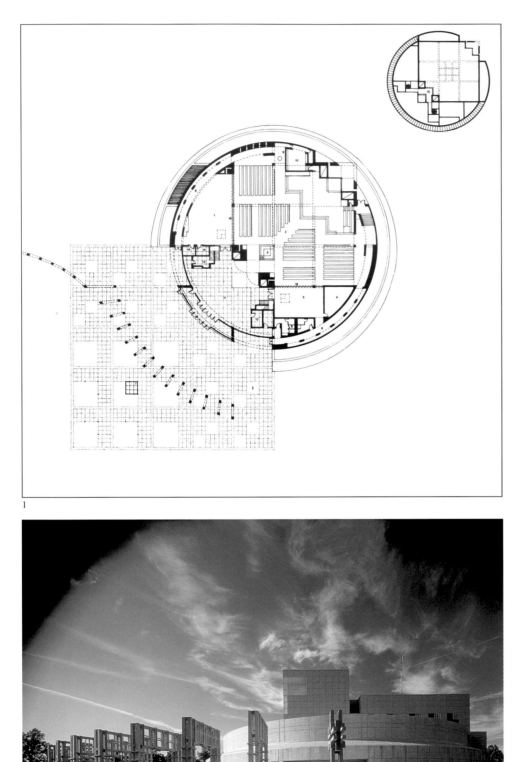

1

2

Providing a "place of discovery for pilgrims" was the primary goal of this indoor worship space, designed to contribute to the pilgrim's sense of a common humanity and belief in God. The church complements the shrine's 6,200-seat outdoor amphitheater, which hosts liturgies and special events during good weather.

Set on a plinth at the edge of a meadow, the church is created from a series of intersecting geometries along a diagonal axis. The circular form of the main church is overlapped on one edge by the square gridded terrace that flows to the interior to form the gathering space. The sanctuary overlaps the opposite edge of the circle and creates a higher cubic massing.

The church's highest form is a tower element that coincides with the overlap of the sanctuary and terrace. Within this footprint is the water font (massive stone ledges) with a small balcony loft above, together serving as the architectural punctuation and the entry into the primary worship space.

1   Site plan
2   South elevation
3   Primary worship area
4   View toward altar
5   Main entry showing "Pilgrim's Gate" trellis

3

4

5

Danforth Chapel

Design/Completion 1997/1997
St. Louis, Missouri, U.S.A.
Sally and Jack Danforth
512 square feet
Wood structure, post and beam with scissor-trusses for roof
Western red cedar siding and cedar shakes, walnut pews and altar

1

1   Aerial view of model
2   View from west
3   View from northeast
4   View of altar
5   Floor plan
6   Section

2

The creation of a simple family chapel for 24 worshippers on a site perched at the edge of a large field and surrounded by rolling hills was the design goal. The design negotiates a middle ground between the Danforth family's home and the expanse of open field separating it from the chapel.

A grove of pine trees to the south shelters and secures the chapel. Western red cedar siding and cedar shakes on the roof have a natural finish. The altar faces east and the entry is to the west. Low trusses at the entry rise gradually toward the chapel's altar end. This change in height creates a curved roof form on the outside and adds height at the altar end of the interior. Abundant windows on both sides admit natural light and improve ventilation. The pews and cross are made from walnut trees from the site.

3

4

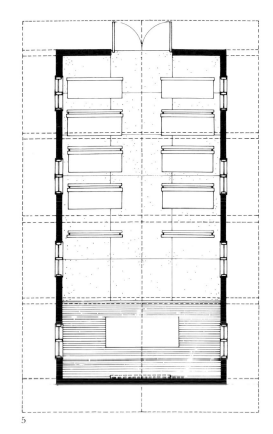

5

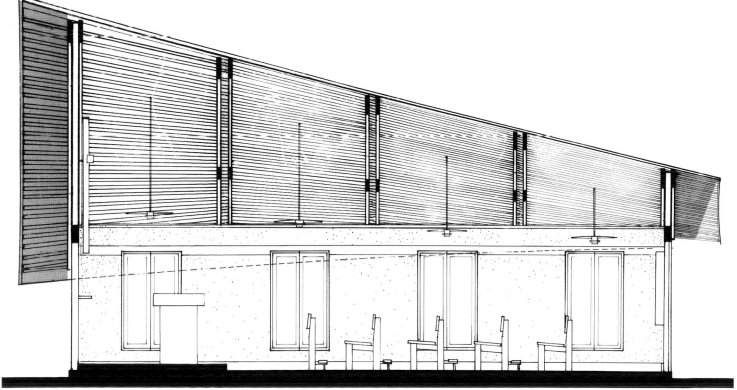

6

Reorganized Church of Jesus Christ of Latter Day Saints World Headquarters

Design/Completion 1988/1993
Independence, Missouri, U.S.A.
Reorganized Church of Jesus Christ of Latter Day Saints
130,000 square feet
Steel structure
Granite, clerestory glass, steel

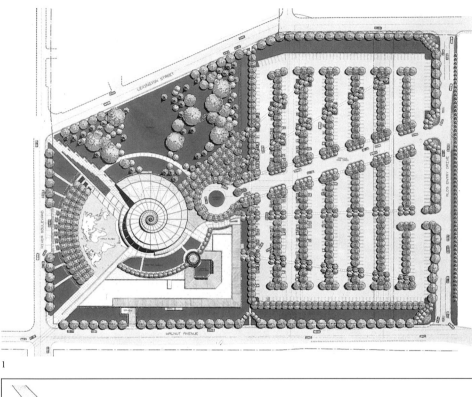

The expression of growth, dynamism, unity, and an international presence were important goals in the design of this temple and world headquarters for the Reorganized Church of Jesus Christ of Latter Days Saints (RLDS).

Inspiring the architecture was the intricate spiral of the nautilus seashell, a form governed by the same natural laws that shape the human umbilical cord, rams' horns, and nebulas found in space. As a symbol of nature found all over the world and in many different cultures, the spiral seemed a fitting symbol of RLDS's worldwide presence.

The 200-foot base creates a sense of intimacy by seating more than 1,600 people in a circular arrangement. From the base, the temple tapers toward the sky to form a spire that peaks at 300 feet. The whirls broaden in a geometric progression, each revolution of the spiral generating an upward and uplifting focus.

1

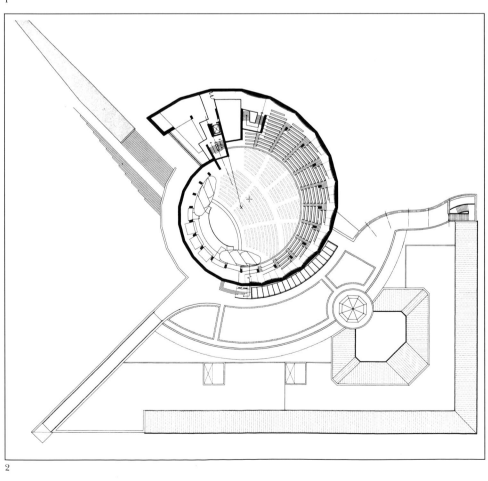

2

1 Site plan
2 Main floor plan
Opposite:
    Entrance to main sanctuary

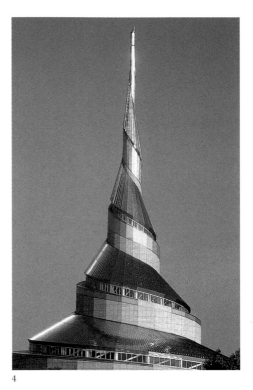

4

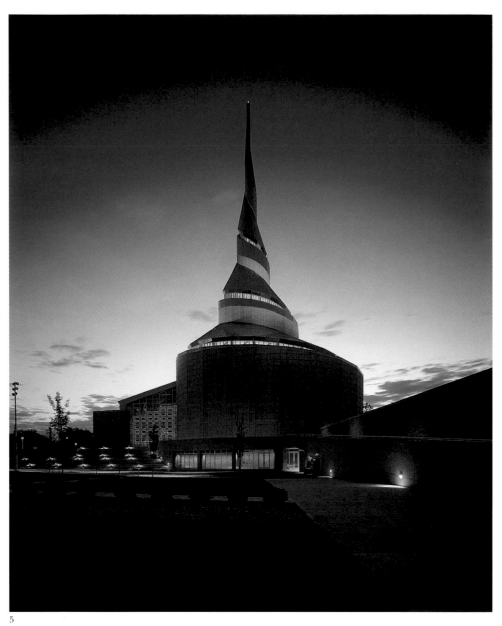

5

4   View of nautilus shell-shaped spire
5   Main entrance at dusk
Opposite:
    Main sanctuary

7

8

9

7 Interior of spire
8 Worshipper's path
9 Sanctuary looking into spire
Opposite:
   Stained glass window on worshipper's path

Thanks to The Images Publishing Group for inviting HOK to update this book for its second printing. We are pleased to have this opportunity to share our latest work and to express our profound appreciation for our clients.

I believe we have the strongest client list in the profession. Over the past half century the brilliant people in these organizations have inspired and challenged HOK's people to do great work. These clients have fueled HOK's growth from a small Midwestern practice into one of the world's largest, most diverse design firms. They're the sole reason we exist, and not a day goes by that we are not grateful.

On behalf of HOK, I would like to thank our clients for:

- Giving our people opportunities to undertake stimulating work

- Entrusting us to create wonderful environments for work, play, healing, worship, scientific discovery, learning, travel—the list goes on

- Pushing us to deliver innovative solutions

- Challenging us to work faster, better, and smarter

- Helping us to make our projects more sustainable

- Building deep, long-term personal and professional relationships with our people

- Feeding our entrepreneurial spirits

HOK's strength—and the key to our future success—is our ability to understand clients: what they want, need, and can afford. We believe that truly listening to clients, and then responding to what we hear, generates inspiring architecture that enriches people's lives.

Bill Valentine, FAIA
President
HOK Group, Inc.

Gyo Obata, FAIA
Founding Partner

Since HOK's founding in 1955, Gyo Obata has been the firm's design inspiration. Today, he continues as a principal designer on key projects while helping with several others. Mr. Obata shares his wisdom with HOK's new and emerging global network of designers. He follows the philosophy of "designing from the inside out," and believes that the final evaluation of any building must be in terms of human values. His designs have received numerous awards from the American Institute of Architects, the U.S. General Services Administration, the Institute of Business Designers and the Federal Design Council.

In addition to many milestone HOK projects, Mr. Obata has designed federal courthouses in St. Louis and Denver, headquarters buildings for Kellogg Company, Levi Strauss, the Reorganized Church of Latter Day Saints and the Federal Reserve Bank of Minneapolis, and the Abraham Lincoln Presidential Library and Museum.

William E. Valentine, FAIA
President

Mr. Valentine is responsible for the firm's overall strategic direction, with an emphasis on ensuring continued design excellence. Mr. Valentine has been an HOK design leader since joining the firm in 1962. Most recently, he served as chair of the HOK Design Board, made up of design directors from the firm's offices worldwide, and Director of Design for HOK's San Francisco office, the firm's oldest office outside its headquarters in St. Louis. Mr. Valentine has designed hundreds of HOK projects.

A compelling and collegial leader, Mr. Valentine is recognized for his ability to fully understand, formulate, and respond to client needs in a creative, individualistic, and people-oriented manner. He has led design efforts in many high-profile HOK projects including King Khaled International Airport, Riyadh, Saudi Arabia; Levi's Plaza, San Francisco, California; Apple Computer's R&D Campus, Cupertino, California; the Scott M. Matheson Courthouse, Salt Lake City, Utah; Nortel Networks Carling R&D Campus Expansion, Ottawa, Ontario, Canada; and the IDEC World Headquarters, San Diego, California.

Tom Boshaw, AIA
Senior Vice President, Design Director, HOK Hong Kong

As Design Director for the Hong Kong office of HOK, Mr. Boshaw has been involved in the design of some of HOK's most prestigious projects in Asia. His international portfolio is filled with high-profile residential, corporate, aviation, office, mixed-use and new town developments. Among these are the China Resources Peak Road Residential Development in Hong Kong; Huaqiang Mixed-Use Development in Shenzhen; McKinley Towers in Fort Bonifacio, Philippines; and Asian Star Office Building in Manila, Philippines.

Steven Christopher Carver
Senior Principal, HOK Sport + Venue + Event

Mr. Carver's design leadership is evident in many award-winning stadiums and arenas. A founding senior principal of HOK Sport + Venue + Event, Mr. Carver has been involved in nearly every aspect of the design process, including programming, site studies, master planning, design, production of contract documents, contract administration, and post-occupancy evaluation. His design efforts include Reliant Stadium in Houston, Texas; Philips Arena in Atlanta, Georgia; Pepsi Center in Denver, Colorado; United Center in Chicago, Illinois; and Gaylord Entertainment Center in Nashville, Tennessee.

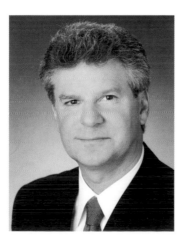

Ernest Cirangle, AIA
Senior Vice President, Design Principal, HOK Los Angeles

Mr. Cirangle, Director of Design for the Los Angeles office of HOK, has 30 years experience in office, hotel, airport, health care, laboratory and urban design projects. Current work includes the LAC + USC Hospital in Los Angeles and the Sciences Building at Cal State San Bernardino. Previously, he was Director of Design for HOK's Hong Kong office, where he was instrumental in the success of the firm's Asia Pacific practice. His international design experience includes JTC Summit Headquarters, Jurong East, Singapore; Sendai International Airport Terminal Building, Sendai, Japan; and Tokyo Telecom Center, Tokyo, Japan.

Jean Michel Colonnier
Senior Associate, Director of Architecture, HOK Mexico

Born and educated in Canada, Mr. Colonnier has practiced for the last eight years in Mexico City. As Director of Architecture for the Mexico City office of HOK, Mr. Colonnier has been influential in transforming corporate office design by applying a strict design methodology which he honed in Canada, and where his work was recognized by *Ordre des Architectes du Quebec* and *Progressive Architecture Magazine* (Award of Excellence). Recent projects include a number of office buildings in Mexico City: Palmas 140, Insurgentes 881, Barranca del Muerto, Punta Santa Fe, and Intelicorp; as well as the CentroAmericas Building in San Salvador, El Salvador; and the Faria Lima Financial Center in Sao Paulo, Brazil.

Chip Crawford, ASLA
Senior Vice President, Director, The HOK Planning Group

Mr. Crawford has over 20 years experience in landscape architecture, planning, and urban design, including national and international master planning experience for corporate, municipal, commercial, health care and resort clients. He has led and participated in numerous award-winning projects, including Confluence Greenway, Gateway Parks and Trails 2004, Chouteau Lake District, St. Louis County Police and Firefighter Memorial Plaza, Clayton, Missouri; Centennial City Master Development Plan, Manila, Philippines; and Stella Maris Monastery, Haifa, Israel.

Kenneth Drucker, AIA
Senior Principal, Director of Design, HOK New York

During his four years as Director of Design for the New York office of HOK, Mr. Drucker has directed the design of many of the firm's recent benchmark projects. His diverse, high-profile clients include MasterCard International, Amtrak, Bristol-Myers Squibb, Tishman-Speyer, the Rockefeller Group, the Toronto Hospital, Rockefeller University, Brown Brothers Harriman, and the New York City Economic Development Corporation. He has been the recipient of some of the architectural world's most prestigious awards including the GSA Design Award, the AIA Honor Award for Urban Design, and New York City's Art Commission.

William Hellmuth, AIA
Senior Principal, Director of Design, HOK Washington, D.C.

With more than 20 years experience in architecture and design, Mr. Hellmuth serves as the Director of the HOK Washington, D.C. design studio. Mr. Hellmuth has achieved a reputation with clients and within the profession for architectural creativity and excellence through superlative client service and a noteworthy portfolio of local, regional, national and international projects. His projects, which have earned numerous Merit Awards from the American Institute of Architects, include the U.S. Embassy, Moscow, Russia; IRS Martinsburg Computing Center, Martinsburg, West Virginia; College Park Aviation Museum, College Park, Maryland; and Irian Jaya Museum & Guest House at Timika, Irian Jaya, Indonesia.

Paul Henry, RAIA
Senior Principal, HOK Sport + Venue + Event

Mr. Henry directs the Asian arm of HOK Sport + Venue + Event from the Brisbane headquarters in Australia. An experienced designer of stadia, arenas, racecourses and overlay, Mr. Henry leads the management and design process of all major projects in Asia. He also advises government and private consortia on the management of the procurement process and the design of sports facilities to best suit a city or country's need. Clients include the 2008 Beijing Olympic Committee, Sydney 2000 Olympic Committee, Hong Kong Jockey Club, Jiangsu Provincial Government of China, and Taipei City Government.

Steven R. Janeway, AIA
Vice President, Director of Design, HOK Dallas

Mr. Janeway has a wide range of design experience, including regional and global projects within the telecommunications, technology and professional service sectors, as well as public and institutional projects such as museums, foreign embassies, university sports venues and dormitories. Recent projects include CentroAmericas in San Salvador, El Salvador; national representation of Ernst & Young, LLP in multiple locations throughout Southeast and Southwest United States; the Alcatel USA campus; the Houston Metro Rail System station designs, Houston, Texas; and President Enterprise Tower in Taipei, Taiwan.

Hal Kantner
Senior Vice President, Director of Visual Communications

With more than 20 years practical and professional experience, Mr. Kantner is a resourceful designer with a proven track record of developing the programs and strategies required by market objectives on a local, national, and international level. During his tenure, HOK Visual Communications has received more than 40 design awards. His expertise is in the design of communications regarding architecture, facilities, workplace and the built environment. He is a specialist in Experienced Enhanced Environments™, marrying visual communications with cultural attributes to create scripted, on-brand architectural experiences.

Lawrence Malcic, AIA
Senior Vice President, Director of Design, HOK London

Mr. Malcic works with clients and colleagues establishing strategic design goals for projects and structuring the design process to fulfill them. His approach is informed by 25 years professional and academic experience that includes teaching in architecture schools and serving as assistant dean of a leading American business school. Examples of his work are the Hilton Metropole Hotel and St. Barnabas Church, London; Passenger Terminal Amsterdam; and Barclays World Headquarters, Canary Wharf. In 2001, 40 Grosvenor Place, London, designed by Mr. Malcic and his colleagues, was chosen "Best Commercial Workplace in Britain."

Sandra Mendler, AIA
Vice President, HOK Sustainable Design Principal

Ms. Mendler is a veteran designer, first with HOK's Washington, D.C. office and currently with the San Francisco office. Since 1992, Ms. Mendler has been integrally involved with the development and implementation of the HOK sustainable design program, including co-authoring *The HOK Guidebook to Sustainable Design*, and establishing numerous other tools and resources. Global Green USA gave HOK its 2001 "Designing a Sustainable and Secure World" award. Sandra is also the recipient of the 2001 "Sustainable Design Leadership Award" by IIDA and Collins and Aikman. Projects include the EPA Environmental Research Center, Research Triangle Park, North Carolina; the World Resources Institute Headquarters Office, Washington, D.C.; and the National Wildlife Federation Headquarters Building, Reston, Virginia.

Ali Moghaddasi
Senior Vice President, Director of Design, HOK Aviation

An 18-year veteran of HOK, Mr. Moghaddasi is the Director of Design for the firm's Aviation Group. Previously he was Co-Director of Design for the San Francisco office of HOK. His aviation experience includes San Francisco International Airport Boarding Area G; King Abdulaziz International Airport in Saudi Arabia; Oakland International Airport, Oakland, California; Delta Air Lines Terminal at JFK International Airport, New York; and Delta Air Lines Terminal A Redevelopment at Boston Logan International Airport, Boston, Massachusetts. Other recent work includes the Novell Corporate Campus, San Jose, California; VERITAS World Headquarters, Mountain View, California; Samsung Research & Development project, Korea; and Mulia Hotel Senayan, a five-star hotel in Jakarta, Indonesia.

William Odell, AIA
Group Vice President and Director of Science + Technology, HOK St. Louis; HOK Sustainable Design Principal

Mr. Odell has been a design principal in the St. Louis office of HOK for many years. For the last three years, he has directed the HOK Science + Technology Group, which specializes in the design of research facilities and other high-performance buildings. Mr. Odell also helps direct HOK's sustainable design effort, and has co-authored two books on sustainable design, including *The HOK Guidebook to Sustainable Design*. He is a frequent speaker on design, sustainable design and the future of the profession. Recent work includes the Federal Reserve Bank of Minneapolis, Minneapolis, Minnesota; Sigma-Aldrich Life Science Technology Center, St. Louis, Missouri; the new Mary Ann Cofrin Hall at the University of Wisconsin – Green Bay; and a new incubator laboratory at the University of Illinois.

Rod Sheard, RIBA, RAIA
Senior Principal, HOK Sport + Venue + Event

Rod Sheard directs the European arm of HOK Sport + Venue + Event from the London headquarters. He has been directing teams in sports, leisure, and entertainment architecture for more than 25 years. Recent works include Stadium Australia, Wembley National Stadium and the RIBA award-winning Alfred McAlpine Stadium in Huddersfield, England. Mr. Sheard is renowned not only for his distinctive design style, but also his visionary outlook on the future of sports architecture, which he frequently shares in books and lectures. His book *Sports Architecture* provides insight and information about sports facility design processes.

Roger M. Soto, AIA
Principal, Director of Design, HOK Houston

Mr. Soto is currently the Director of Design for the Houston office of HOK where he oversees a diversified practice in corporate, health care, and higher education facilities. Prior to this assignment, Mr. Soto helped establish HOK's first Latin American office based in Mexico City. During the last few years, his work has focused primarily on corporate/commercial architecture, including projects such as Tivoli Systems Headquarters Campus, Austin, Texas; Calpine Tower in downtown Houston, Texas; and the new corporate campus for USAA, Phoenix, Arizona.

Joseph Spear, AIA
Senior Principal, HOK Sport + Venue + Event

Mr. Spear, a founding senior principal of HOK Sport + Venue + Event, is one of the world's most accomplished ballpark designers. His experience has included site studies, master planning, design, cost estimating, delineation of design concepts, and contract administration. He led the design of Oriole Park at Camden Yards and Jacobs Field, the only two ballparks to be awarded National AIA Honor Awards for Architecture. Mr. Spear's design direction has also influenced such projects as Great American Ballpark in Cincinnati, Ohio; Pacific Bell Park in San Francisco, California; Comerica Park in Detroit, Michigan; and Coors Field in Denver, Colorado.

Gordon Stratford
Vice President, Director of Design, HOK Toronto

Mr. Stratford's 20 years experience in architecture and interior design is distinguished by many award-winning projects. As Director of Design for the Toronto office of HOK, Mr. Stratford utilizes his extensive experience in corporate and high-tech projects for clients such as Nortel Networks, GE Capital ITS, and Netscape Canada. He serves as the prime design liaison between client groups and other consultants, and is responsible for the overview, supervision, and execution of major design projects and presentations.

Marek Tryzybowicz
Vice President, Director of Design, HOK Berlin/Warsaw

With HOK since 1989, Mr. Tryzybowicz has extensive award-winning international experience in designing for mixed-use retail, planning, and corporate clients. Representative projects include Galeria Mokotów and Wilanow Masterplan, Warsaw, Poland; Sony Music European Corporate Headquarters, and German Railways Corporate Headquarters, Berlin, Germany; Mall of Taiwan, Chung Li, Taiwan; Marina Town Center, Fukuoka, Japan; Exxon Mobil World Headquarters, Irving, Texas; and Oryx Energy Company, Dallas, Texas. As Director of Design for the HOK Berlin and Warsaw offices, and a member of the HOK Design Board, Mr. Tryzybowicz sets design directions for projects, formulates design concepts, and assures quality design solutions.

Yann R. Weymouth, AIA
Senior Vice President, Director of Design, HOK Tampa

As Director of Design for the Tampa office of HOK, Mr. Weymouth brings more than 33 years experience in design and project management to HOK's Florida practice. He was chief design architect for the Louvre Museum in Paris under I.M. Pei, and held the same role for the East Wing of the National Gallery in Washington, D.C. Recent experience includes the expansion and renovation of the John & Mable Ringling Museum in Sarasota, Florida; the renovation of the Metropolitan Museum of Art, New York; and the Hialeah City Courthouse, Miami.

Henry T. Winkelman, AIA
Group Vice President, Director of Design, HOK Health Care

Mr. Winkelman has been directing the design efforts on major clinical research and health care, mixed-use, and institutional projects since he joined HOK in 1981. His wealth of experience allows him to expertly manage and lead colleagues and clients alike with a style of collaboration and interaction. Recent projects include BJC HealthCare, St. Louis, Missouri; Northwestern Memorial Hospital, Chicago, Illinois; New York Presbyterian Hospital, New York, New York; and University of Alabama Birmingham Hospital, Birmingham, Alabama.

Paul S. Woolford, AIA
Senior Vice President, Director of Design, HOK Atlanta

Mr. Woolford has 20 years experience in the practice of university, corporate, research, hospitality, and transportation architecture, as well as urban design and planning. Mr. Woolford has been responsible for some of the largest and most complex buildings completed by the firm. His designs include Shelby Hall, the Interdisciplinary Science Building at the University of Alabama, Tuscaloosa; the Whitehead Biomedical Research Facility at Emory University, Atlanta, Georgia; the College of Medicine for Florida State University, Tallahassee, Florida; and a new facility for the State of Georgia Department of Archives and History.

Steven Worthington, AIA
Senior Vice President, Director of Design, HOK San Francisco

As a 22-year veteran of HOK, Mr. Worthington has contributed to the design vision of many of HOK's most prominent corporate facilities. His success comes from an ingenuity and energy that he brings to the design process, attention to detail, interpersonal skills and sensitivity to control the budget and schedule. Mr. Worthington's portfolio features national and international clients such as Visa U.S.A., Adobe, Advanced Micro Devices, Microsoft, Fairmont Hotels, Nortel Networks, Fukuoka International Airport, Fukuoka, Japan, and many private developers, including Boston Properties, Equity Office, Hines, Shorenstein, and Tishman Speyer.

Management Teams for Offices and Markets

Atlanta
David Hronek
Karen League
Mike Miller
Dick Scharf
Paul Woolford

Berlin
Michael Lees

Brisbane
See Sport + Venue + Event

Canada
Terry Comeau
Lui Mancinelli
Gordon Stratford

Chicago
See St. Louis/Chicago

Dallas
Keith Bowman
Steven Janeway
Kirk Millican
Sandra Paret

Florida
Duncan Broyd
Beth Bernitt
Chris Osborn
Yann Weymouth

Hong Kong
Tom Boshaw
Shupai Koo

Houston
Ed Abboud
Cathy Britt
Ford Hubbard
Gary Kuzma
Molly McIntyre-Hair
Robert Mease
Tom Robson
Roger Soto

Kansas City
See Sport + Venue + Event

London
Pierre Baillargeon
Andrew Barraclough
Ralph Courtenay
Larry Malcic
Riccardo Mascia
Paul Purvis
Alexander Redgrave
Richard Spencer
Sinclair Webster
See also Sport + Venue + Event

Los Angeles
Ernest Cirangle
John Conley
Susan Grossinger
Paul Thometz

Mexico City
Jean Michel Colonnier
Juan Carlos Jimenez
Arturo PerezRivera
Juan Andres Vergara

New York
Kenneth Drucker
Juliette Lam
Chuck Siconolfi
Sam Spata

St. Louis/Chicago
Jim Adkins
Nora Akerberg
Bob Blaha
David Chassin
Clark Davis
Paul DeCelles
Steve Evans
Michael Frawley
Gerry Gilmore
Tom Goulden
Debra Handy
Tom Kaczkowski
Tish Kruse
Dennis Laflen
Penny Malina
Roger McFarland
Everett Medling
Bill Odell
Ripley Rasmus
Kyle St. Peter
Bob Schwartz
Mike Stern
Paul Strohm
Henry Winkelman

San Francisco
Ed McCrary
Steve Worthington

Warsaw
Marek Tryzybowicz

Washington, D.C.
Robert Barr
Robert Cox
George Hellmuth
William Hellmuth
James Kessler
Susan Klumpp Williams
Elizabeth Peterson
Christopher Ryan
William Stinger

Aviation
Pat Askew
Michael DeBernard
Darryl McDonald
Ali Moghaddasi

Conservation
Neil Cooke

Consulting
Ann Althoff
Steve Morton
Hugh Painter
Steve Parshall

Corporate Services
Ann Althoff
David Whiteman

Design + Build
Clark Davis
Michael Newland
Michael Rallo

Engineering
Edmond Abboud
Jim Adkins
Guy Despatis
Saed Dimachkieh
Gary Kuzma
Dick Powers
Dave Troup

Health Care
Richard Saravay
Chuck Siconolfi
Paul Strohm
Henry Winkelman

Interiors
Beth Bernitt
Juliette Lam
Susan Grossinger
Roger McFarland
Sandra Paret

Justice
Duncan Broyd
John Eisenlau
Michael Frawley
Jim Kessler
Chuck Oraftik
Bill Prindle
Bob Schwartz
Charles Smith
Ed Spooner

Planning
Bob Belden
Chip Crawford
Sara Liss-Katz
Bill Palmer
Monte Wilson

Program Management
Douglas Dodds
David Kusturin
Julius Gombos

Retail
Pierre Baillargeon
Tony Greenland
Joe Pettipas
Marek Tryzybowicz
Philip Wren

Science + Technology
George Hellmuth
Dave Hronek
Sandy Mendler
Bill Odell
Sam Spata

Sport + Venue + Event
Ben Barnert
John Barrow
Steven Christopher Carver
Randy Dvorak
Paul Henry
Rick Martin
Scott Radecic
Earl Santee
Rod Sheard
Joseph Spear
Todd Voth
Jim Walters
Dennis Wellner

Transportation
Kirk Millican
Kent Turner

Visual Communications
Mark Askew
Craig Hein
Hal Kantner

Office Locations

Atlanta
235 Peachtree Street NE, Suite 500
Atlanta, GA 30303 USA
404 439 9000

Berlin
Kantstr. 17
D-10623 Berlin, Germany
49 30 243 1400

Brisbane
HOK S+V+E
40 Edward Street
P.O. Box 216 Albert Street
Brisbane QLD 4002 Australia
617 3210 2530

Chicago
30 West Monroe Street, Suite 1500
Chicago, IL 60603 USA
312 782 1000

Dallas
2001 Ross Avenue, Suite 2800
Lock Box 106
Dallas, TX 75201 USA
214 720 6000

Hong Kong
24/F Kinwick Centre
32 Hollywood Road
Central, Hong Kong
852 2534 0000

Houston
2800 Post Oak Boulevard, Suite 3700
Houston, TX 77056 USA
713 407 7700

Kansas City
HOK S+V+E
323 West 8th Street, Suite 700
Kansas City, MO 64105 USA
816 221 1500

Kansas City
HOK Design+Build
323 West 8th Street, Suite 106
Kansas City, MO 64105 USA
816 421 0202

London
216 Oxford Street
London W1C 1DB England
44 (0)20 7636 2006

London
HOK S+V+E
HOK Sport Limited
14 Blades Court
London SW 15 2NU England
44 (0)20 8874 7666

Los Angeles
9530 Jefferson Boulevard
Culver City, CA 90232 USA
310 838 9555

Mexico City
Paseo de la Reforma 265, MZ1
Colonia Cuauhtémoc
06500 México, DF
52 (55) 52 0 80 801

New York
620 Avenue of the Americas
New York, NY 10011 USA
212 741 1200

Orlando
300 South Orange Avenue, Suite 1150
Orlando, FL 32801 USA
407 649 8825

Ottawa
HOK Canada, Inc.
1770 Woodward Drive, Suite 200
Ottawa, ON K2C 0P8 Canada
613 226 9650

St. Louis
211 North Broadway, Suite 600
St. Louis, MO 63102 USA
314 421 2000

San Francisco
One Bush Street, Suite 200
San Francisco, California 94104 USA
415 243 0555

Tampa
One Tampa City Center, Suite 3000
Tampa, FL 33602 USA
813 229 0300

Toronto
HOK Canada, Inc.
Suite 802, P.O. Box 105
207 Queen's Quay West
Toronto, ON M5J 1A7 Canada
416 203 9993

Toronto
PMGlobal
121 King Street West, Suite 2130
P.O. Box 21
Toronto, ON M5H 3T9 Canada
416 203 4700

Warsaw
ul. Foksal 19
00-372 Warsaw, Poland
48 22 827 9277

Washington, DC
Canal House
3223 Grace Street, N.W.
Washington, DC 20007 USA
202 339 8700

Acknowledgments

I am a hopeless fan of HOK: our clients, our people, our work, and our future. Because of that, selecting the projects to include in this book truly was a labor of love. The process was time-consuming and, at times, difficult. It seemed that every project we included had a just-as-deserving counterpart that space limitations forced us to leave out.

But the process also gave me an opportunity to fall in love again with our work. I'm so excited and proud to see how our people are using great design to solve problems.

I'm especially beholden to HOK's amazing group of clients. I know in my heart that we have the best client list in the industry.

Thanks to the Images Publishing Group for inviting us to update this book for its second printing. And thanks to our talented network of designers and the industrious people in HOK's Communications group for making this book happen.

When I joined HOK in 1962, we had 50 people. What immediately struck me about the firm was the eagerness of our people to enhance lives through design. We were encouraged to take responsibility and given the freedom we needed to succeed.

Today, though we've grown to a firm of almost 2,000 people, the desire to use design to improve the human condition still permeates HOK. The only difference is that we're involved in an enormous array of work in almost every region of the world. The opportunities for taking responsibility are immense – and that invigorates us all.

Bill Valentine, FAIA
President
HOK Group, Inc.

Photography Credits

Russell Abraham
118 (1, 2); 119 (3, 4)

Aker/Zvonkovic Photography
125 (1,3); 156 (1, 2); 157 (3,4)

Peter Aaron
7 (Stanford University Library); 74 (1, 2,); 140 (2); 141 (4)

Farshid Assassi
60 (1); 61 (2,3,4); 139 (VERITAS Software Headquarters Campus)

Robert Azzi
106 (4); 107 (5); 116 (1, 3); 117 (4, 5)

Nathen Benn
8 (NASM); 214 (3)

Patrick Bingham-Hall
62 (1); 63 (2,3,4); 70 (1,2); 71 (3,4); 72 (5,6)

Craig Blackmon
124 (3, 4, 5)

David Carrico
198 (2)

Dixie Carrillo
142 (2); 197 (1,2)

Colin Goldie Photography
206 (1)

Peter Cook
35 (Maiashopping); 36 (2, 3); 50 (4); 51 (5,6); 52 (2,4); 168 (2); 169 (4); 210 (1, 2, 3); 211 (4); 212 (5,6) 228 (1,2) 229 (4, 5)

George Cott
9 (Tampa Convention Center); 14 (2); 15 (4); 38 (1, 2); 75 (1, 2); 94 (1, 3); 95 (4); 105 (Orlando International Airport Airside 2); 155 (2,3); 215 (4); 222 (2); 223 (3, 4)

Craig Dugan
183 (6)

Peter Durrant
244 (1,2)

Bob Freund
127 (1,2)

Yukio Futagawa
112 (2, 3, 4); 113 (5, 6); 114 (7)

Jeff Goldberg
9 (Oriole Park at Camden Yards)

Bob Greenspan
57 (2,3,4)

Tim Griffith
34 (1,2,3,4); 110 (2); 111 (3,4,5,6); 150 (2) 160 (1,2); 161 (3,4,6)

Steve Hall @ Hedrich Blessing
92 (5, 6); 162 (2); 164 (5); 165 (7); 166 (8)

Chris Hayne
115 (Whitehead Biomedical Research Building at Emory University)

Hedrich Blessing Photography
93 (2,3); 99 (4)

Jonathan Hillyer Photography inc.
128 (4)

Timothy Hursley
11 (Tokyo Telecom); 47 (3); 48 (5); 73 (Anaheim Convention Center Expansion); 76 (1); 78 (6); 80 (2); 81 (3,4,5,6); 96 (1); 97 (5); 98 (6,7,8,9); 99 (1,3,); 102 (2); 103 (3, 4, 5); 108 (2); 109 (3,4,5); 128 (3); 158 (1, 2); 159 (4); 185 (2,4)

Kerun Ip
170 (1,2); 171 (2,3); 174 (1); 175 (3,4); 199 (One McKinley)

Alan Karchmer
86 (1,2,3); 87 (4); 133 (4)

Balthazar Korab
10 (RLDS); 10 (Florida Aquarium); 41 (3, 4); 42 (5, 6,); 43 (7); 120 (1); 76 (2); 77 (4, 5); 120 (1); 121 (3,5,6); 220 (1,2); 230 (2); 231 (3, 4, 5); 235 (3,4); 236 (4, 5); 237 (6); 238 (7, 8, 9); 239 (10)

Brian Kuhlmann
77 (3)

Michael Lewis
56 (1)

Daniela MacAdden
176 (1,2); 177 (3)

Ed Massery
53 (Heinz Field)

Mitsuo Matsuoka/Koji Kobayashi
200 (2,3); 201 (5,6,7)

Scott McDonald @ Hedrich Blessing
154 (2,3,4); 182 (4,); 183 (5); 184 (7,8)

Chas McGrath
11 (Nortel Brampton Centre); 150 (3)

Peter Mealin Photography
26 (1); 27 (3,4)

Nick Merrick @ Hedrich Blessing
28 (1, 2, 3); 29 (4); 30 (5, 6, 7); 31 (8); 85 (Utah Consolidated Courts Complex); 104 (1,2,4); 147 (3,5); 148 (3,4); 149 (3,4); 152 (2); 153 (3,4); 178 (1,2)

Gregory Murphey
82 (1); 83 (2,3,4) 106 (3); 107 (6)

Paul Nagashima
219 (4)

Alise O'Brien
136 (3, 4); 137 (6, 7); 232 (2, 3); 233 (4)

Peter Paige
144 (1,2,3,4); 145 (7,8)

Robert Pettus
8 (Metropolitan Square); 39 (4, 5, 6); 208 (2); 218 (3); 219 (5,6,7)

Erhard Pfeiffer
122 (2, 3); 123 (4, 5, 6)

Andrzej Pisarski
37 (2,3,4)

Gary Quesada
150 (1); 151 (4)

Marvin Rand
48 (6);

Christian Richters
16 (3); 17 (4,5,6), 18

Rion Rizzo
66 (1,2,3) 67 (4); 134 (1,2,3)

George Silk
6 (Priory Chapel); 7 (Dallas/Ft. Worth International Airport); 14 (3); 130 (2); 141 (3, 5); 214 (2); 216 (5); 226 (2); 227 (3, 4, 5)

John Sutton
142 (, 3, 4); 143 (5) 146 (2); 147 (4)

David Whittaker
186 (3)

Don Wong
88 (2); 89 (3); 90, 91 (4); 92 (7)

Roy Wright
131 (5); 136 (5); 138 (8)

Ken Wyner
129 (Johns Hopkins Asthma and Allergy Center)

Rendering Credits

Anderson Terzie Partnership
168 (3)

David Carrico
192 (2); 193 (1,3)

Glowfrog Studios
203 (2)

Interface Multimedia
217 (1,2,3)

Laura Linn
192 (3); 193 (1,3); 221 (1); 127 (4)

Doug Jamieson
181 (4); 188 (1,3,4)

Michael Morrissey
206 (4)

Steve Parker
20 (2); 21 (4,5); 25 (2); 33 (3,4); 185 (3); 193 (2); 194 (2); 221 (2)

David Pentland
44 (1)

Ian Pentland
25 (1)

Michael Sechman
173 (1)

David Span
187 (7)

Index

Every effort has been made to trace the original source of copyright material contained in this book. The publishers would be pleased to hear from copyright holders to rectify any errors or omissions.

The information and illustrations in this publication have been prepared and supplied by Hellmuth, Obata + Kassabaum. While all reasonable efforts have been made to ensure accuracy, the publishers do not, under any circumstances, accept responsibility for errors, omissions and representations express or implied.